Genuine faith

JAMES

by Sam Allberry

thegood**book**
COMPANY

James For You

If you are reading *James For You* alongside this Good Book Guide, here is how the studies in this booklet link to the chapters of *James For You*:

Study One → Ch 1-2   Study Four → Ch 6
Study Two → Ch 3-4   Study Five → Ch 7
Study Three → Ch 5   Study Six → Ch 8-10

In view of God's mercy
The good book guide to Romans 8 – 16
© Timothy Keller, 2015. Reprinted 2017, 2018, 2020, 2021.
Series Consultants: Tim Chester, Tim Thornborough,
                    Anne Woodcock, Carl Laferton

Published by:
The Good Book Company

thegoodbook.com | www.thegoodbook.co.uk
thegoodbook.com.au | thegoodbook.co.nz | thegoodbook.co.in

Unless indicated, all Scripture references are taken from the Holy Bible, New International Version. Copyright © 2011 Biblica, Inc.TM Used by permission.

ISBN: 9781910307816 | Printed in India

CONTENTS

Introduction   **4**

Why study James?   **5**

1. Joy in trials   **7**
James 1 v 1-18

2. Listen well   **13**
James 1 v 19 – 2 v 13

3. Faith works   **19**
James 2 v 14-26

4. Tongues on fire   **25**
James 3 v 1-18

5. How to come back to God   **31**
James 4 v 1-12

6. Wisdom in planning, patience in suffering   **37**
James 4 v 13 – 5 v 20

Leader's Guide   **43**

Introduction: Good Book Guides

Every Bible-study group is different—yours may take place in a church building, in a home or in a cafe, on a train, over a leisurely mid-morning coffee or squashed into a 30-minute lunch break. Your group may include new Christians, mature Christians, non-Christians, mums and tots, students, businessmen or teens. That's why we've designed these *Good Book Guides* to be flexible for use in many different situations.

Our aim in each session is to uncover the meaning of a passage, and see how it fits into the "big picture" of the Bible. But that can never be the end. We also need to appropriately apply what we have discovered to our lives. Let's take a look at what is included:

⊖ **Talkabout:** Most groups need to "break the ice" at the beginning of a session, and here's the question that will do that. It's designed to get people talking around a subject that will be covered in the course of the Bible study.

⊕ **Investigate:** The Bible text for each session is broken up into manageable chunks, with questions that aim to help you understand what the passage is about. The **Leader's Guide** contains **guidance for questions**, and sometimes ⊗ additional "follow-up" questions.

⊕ **Explore more (optional):** These questions will help you connect what you have learned to other parts of the Bible, so you can begin to fit it all together like a jig-saw; or occasionally look at a part of the passage that's not dealt with in detail in the main study.

⊖ **Apply:** As you go through a Bible study, you'll keep coming across **apply** sections. These are questions to get the group discussing what the Bible teaching means in practice for you and your church. ⊙ **Getting personal** is an opportunity for you to think, plan and pray about the changes that you personally may need to make as a result of what you have learned.

⊕ **Pray:** We want to encourage prayer that is rooted in God's word—in line with his concerns, purposes and promises. So each session ends with an opportunity to review the truths and challenges highlighted by the Bible study, and turn them into prayers of request and thanksgiving.

The **Leader's Guide** and introduction provide historical background information, explanations of the Bible texts for each session, ideas for **optional extra** activities, and guidance on how best to help people uncover the truths of God's word.

Why study James?

What should it *look like* to be a Christian? How can I be sure my faith is not just theoretical? What difference should trusting Jesus make to my everyday life?

These questions lie at the heart of the letter of James. James is writing to Christians (like us) who are in danger of making Christianity just a matter of hot air—something we claim to have while actually just living the sort of lives we would have been living if we'd never heard of Jesus. James is wanting Christians to pause and check: *what is genuine faith, and does my life show evidence of it?*

After all, real faith in Jesus is not seen in what we claim, but in how we live. It shows itself in all kinds of real-life ways. James knows what life is like, and so this book is all about showing us what difference real faith makes in the real world. We see how Christians are to respond to suffering and trials, injustice and illness, conflict with others and temptation within. James shows us how to think about everything from poverty and wealth to planning and prayer. He shows us what our hearts and tongues are really like. But more than that, he shows us what our great God is like, and how all we do flows from who he is.

These six studies will help you see the beauty and practicality of genuine Christianity. James' letter is full of vivid imagery and punchy language. He does not beat around the bush. In style as well as content, this is down-to-earth Christianity.

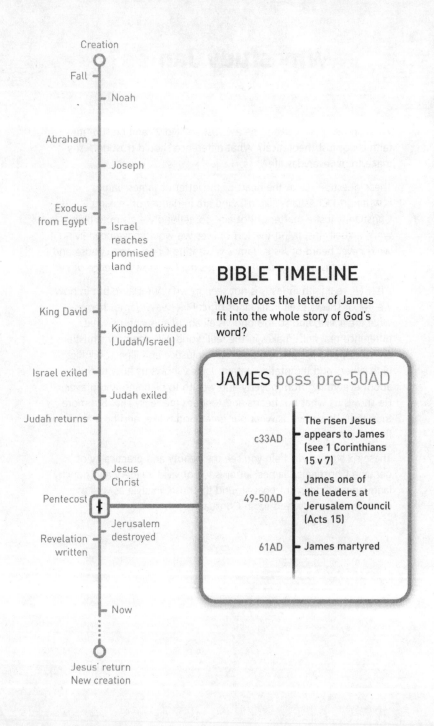

Creation

Fall

Noah

Abraham

Joseph

Exodus
from Egypt

Israel
reaches
promised
land

BIBLE TIMELINE

Where does the letter of James
fit into the whole story of God's
word?

King David

Kingdom divided
(Judah/Israel)

Israel exiled

Judah exiled

Judah returns

JAMES poss pre-50AD

c33AD — The risen Jesus
appears to James
(see 1 Corinthians
15 v 7)

Jesus
Christ

Pentecost

49-50AD — James one of
the leaders at
Jerusalem Council
(Acts 15)

Jerusalem
destroyed

Revelation
written

61AD — James martyred

Now

Jesus' return
New creation

1 James 1 v 1-18
JOY IN TRIALS

⊕ talkabout

1. What do you see as the relationship between joy and suffering? Why?

• How do wealth and poverty usually influence our joy? Why?

⊕ investigate

❯ Read James 1 v 1-12

2. How does James' description of himself and of his readers make reading this letter exciting?

> **DICTIONARY**
>
> **Twelve tribes (v 1):** a term describing the people of God.
> **Trials (v 2):** testing periods of life: persecution, suffering, ill-health, and so on.
> **Perseverance (v 4):** an ability to keep going.
> **Humiliation (v 10):** a process or event that causes someone to think less highly of themselves.
> **Blessed (v 12):** enjoying the satisfaction and security of living the way we were designed to, under God's rule.

3. What kind of person does James want his readers to be, does verse 12 suggest?

4. What is the main way that we can be or become this type of person (v 2)?

- How is this view different from how we tend to view suffering?

- What reasons does James give for viewing suffering in this way (v 3-4)?

5. What should we do if we struggle to have the "wisdom" to look at our trials in this way (v 5)?

- How will God respond (v 5)?

- What warning does James give in v 6-8? How does "double-minded" (v 8) help us to understand what he means by "doubt" in verse 6?

❯ **Read Romans 5 v 1-8**

We are justified through faith (that is, we are declared innocent by God because of Jesus' life and death).

What do we enjoy as a result of this (v 1-2)?
What else do we do, and why (v 3-4)?
How does Paul reassure us this isn't just wishful thinking in:
• v 5?   • v 6-8?
How do Paul's words here reinforce and add to James' message in James 1 v 1-8?

⊡ **apply**

6. How should knowing what Christians will receive in the future (v 12) affect our view of suffering now? What stops us viewing our lives like this?

7. What is attractive about being able to consider trials with "pure joy"?

• How is this a strong witness to those around us?

⊡ getting personal

Is there a trial in your life that you have not been considering as "pure joy"? What stops you thinking of it like that?

What would change in your life overall if you were able to see the trial in a joyful way? What might God be doing in you through that hardship that could begin to help you see it differently?

Would memorising verse 12 help you to change your perspective?

⊡ investigate

8. How should humble (poor) Christians view themselves (v 9-11)? And rich ones? How does the world view these two states differently?

• Why does the gospel encourage the poor, and humble the rich?

Trials around us can prompt all manner of temptations within us. Understanding temptation is therefore vital for ensuring that we respond in healthy ways to the difficult circumstances we often find ourselves in. We need to make sure we are not "deceived" (v 16).

▷ Read James 1 v 13-18

9. Where does temptation *not* come from? Where does it come from (v 13-14)?

DICTIONARY

Enticed (v 14): attracted.
Firstfruits (v 18): the initial batch of a farmer's crop, which proves and guarantees the rest of the harvest is on its way.

• Where does temptation lead, if it is not resisted (v 15)?

10. Temptation does not come from God. What *does* come from him
(v 17-18)?

⊖ apply

11. What are the particular temptations we might face when we feel we are:
• in a period of great trial?

• poor?

• rich?

12. What thought process have verses 13-18 taught us to go through, and encourage others to go through, when temptation comes?

⊡ **getting personal**

Do you need to change your view of relative wealth, and/or of relative poverty? How?

⬆ **pray**

Thank God for his character: the generous, unchanging Father of the heavenly lights.

Thank God for giving you birth through the word of truth, and for promising you a crown of life in eternity.

Share some trials that you are facing, and pray for each other, for wisdom to consider them "pure joy". Then pray for anyone in your church who you know is facing a particularly difficult trial right now.

2 James 1 v 19 – 2 v 13
LISTEN WELL

The story so far

We need to ask for wisdom to know joy and resist temptations in trials, remembering that trials mature us as Christians, and beyond them is eternity.

⊕ talkabout

1. What makes someone a good listener?

⊥ investigate

▶ **Read James 1 v 19-27**

2. What does James say stops someone from being a "good listener" (v 19, 22)?

• What do we do if we listen well to God's word (v 21)?

3. How does the illustration James uses show us the difference between bad listening and good listening (v 23-24)?

4. How does verse 25 motivate us to listen well to God's word?

5. What is the kind of "religion" that pleases God (v 26-27)?

• How does this add to our understanding of what a "good listener" is when it comes to God's word?

⊡ **apply**

6. Why is it very easy to listen to the word wrongly? What ways have you found to keep yourself listening well?

7. If you had to come up with four or five "items of evidence" that show someone is a committed Christian, would you come up with the ones James does in v 19, 21, and 27? Why / why not?

• How does this challenge us about our own Christian lives?

⊡ getting personal

We are right to care about truth and sound doctrine. That is a key outworking of accepting God's word. But there is a danger that we make such understanding an end in itself, rather than a means to the greater end of becoming more like our God in how we look after those in especial need.

As you look at your own life, how does verse 27 encourage you as you see yourself pleasing God in your religion?
How does it challenge you? Do you need to start, or stop, something?
How will you use the knowledge that there is a life that "pleases" God himself to motivate you towards changing?

⊡ investigate

▶ **Read James 2 v 1-13**

8. What is the command (v 1)?

• Can you put James' example in v 2-3 into the context of your own church?

9. Why should Christians not show favouritism?
• v 4

• v 5

• v 6-7

• v 8

10. If a Christian shows favouritism in their treatment of others, how much does it matter whether they're a murderer or adulterer? Why (v 9-11)?

11. How does James want his readers to "speak and act" towards others (v 12-13)? How would this affect their behaviour in the example James gave in v 2-3?

⊡ apply

12. How might you as individuals, in your church, or in wider Christian circles, give priority to those the world sees as "strategic"?

• How does the gospel both challenge you about, and liberate you from, that attitude?

⊡ getting personal

Christians exalting the rich, powerful or impressive goes right against the grain of how God works, and of the gospel itself. God's ways are not the world's ways. Neither should ours be.

What "favouritisms" do you see in your own heart? Think about which members of your church you choose to spend time with; seek wisdom from; wish to imitate.

How will you connect God's treatment of you in the gospel with your treatment of others in your church?

⬆ pray

Give thanks:

- for God's word, and for the freedom that comes from obeying it.
- for God's mercy, and for how that both comforts and humbles you.
- for God's care for the vulnerable.

Pray:

- about areas where you are struggling to obey God's word. Ask him to help you see the freedom and blessedness that will come from obedience.
- that God would show you ways in which you as a church may be showing favouritism that undermines the gospel
- for God's help to love all your neighbours well.

3 James 2 v 14-26
FAITH WORKS

The story so far

We need to ask for wisdom to know joy and resist temptations in trials, remembering that trials mature us as Christians, and beyond them is eternity.

We listen to God well when we don't just hear his word, but obey it—including controlling our speech, caring for the needy, and showing love, not favouritism.

⊕ talkabout

1. How can you tell if someone is a Christian?

⊍ investigate

> **▶ Read James 2 v 14-19**

2. How do James' example and conclusion in verses 15-17 answer his questions in verse 14?

3. In verses 15-16, what is the difference between what this person seems to claim with their words, and actually shows by their actions?

- How would someone with genuine faith have responded in this situation?

In verse 18, James imagines someone objecting like this: *James, there are different types of Christian out there. We don't all have the same approach. We have our own way of living the Christian life. Some are "thinky" types, forever reading up on their doctrine. Then there are more practical types. And that's fine. You've got your faith; I've got my deeds.*

4. But how does James say real faith reveals itself (v 18)?

⊞ **explore more**

▶ **Read Mark 2 v 1-12**

What does Mark tell us Jesus "saw" (v 5)?
How did Jesus react to seeing this (v 5)?
But how was he able to "see" that these men had faith?
How does this underline James' teaching about what genuine faith is?

optional

---

5. What central Christian doctrine does James point to (v 19)? Who does he say is in full agreement on this point?

• What point is he making about faith that is only doctrinal—that is, all about believing the right things?

➔ **apply**

6. What kinds of "counterfeit Christianity" is James warning us about in these verses?

• Why are these forms of false Christianity easier to live out than genuine Christianity?

• How can churches allow or even encourage one another to think these counterfeit "Christianities" are genuine, saving faith?

⊡ **getting personal**

Consider your own faith. Are you in danger of having "mere" sentimental faith, or solely doctrinal faith? What evidence is there in your life to back up your answer?

⊍ investigate

James has shown us two types of counterfeit faith. Next, he gives us two real-life examples of genuine faith.

❯ Read James 2 v 20-26

7. **Read Genesis 15 v 1-6 and 22 v 1-19.** What came first—Abraham obeying God in his actions, or Abraham being made righteous (that is, Abraham being saved)?

> **DICTIONARY**
>
> **Father (v 21):** ancestor.
> **Credited (v 23):** reckoned; given.
> **Righteousness (v 23):** the status of being in right relationship with God.

*   So how were his "faith and his actions ... working together" (James 2 v 22) when he proved willing to sacrifice his son? How was the Scripture of Genesis 15 "fulfilled" at that point?

*   If Abraham had not had genuine faith, how would he have acted differently in Genesis 22?

8. So how do we see whether or not someone is considered righteous by God (James 2 v 24)?

9. Read Joshua 2 v 1-24. How did what Rahab "did" (James 2 v 25) prove that she had genuine faith?

• If Rahab had not had genuine faith, how would she have acted differently in Joshua 2?

10. What do Abraham and Rahab teach us about:

• the relationship between faith (by which James means the claim to be trusting God) and works?

• how you can know whether or not someone (including you) has genuine faith?

⊖ apply

After church one day, a worried-looking friend says she's found a confusing contradiction in the New Testament. First, she points to James 2 v 24. Then she quotes Paul in Romans 3 v 28: "We maintain that a person is justified by faith apart from the works of the law".

11. How would you explain how Paul and James are not disagreeing with each other?

12. How does this passage challenge complacent Christians? How might it encourage concerned Christians?

⊡ getting personal

Can you think of ways in which you have acted differently than you otherwise would have because you trust God's promises and know he has saved you (that is, you have real faith)?

Do you need this passage to challenge you, or to encourage you, do you think? Who could you ask to give you their insight into the genuineness of your faith?

Do you need to ask God, right now, to give you genuine faith?

⬆ pray

Pray, as David did: "Who can discern their own errors? Forgive my hidden faults" (Psalm 19 v 12). Ask him to show you ways in which you may be in danger of counterfeit faith. Then ask him to enable you to be so in love with Jesus that you live as Abraham and Rahab did.

4 James 3 v 1-18
TONGUES ON FIRE

The story so far

We need to ask for wisdom to know joy and resist temptations in trials, remembering that trials mature us as Christians, and beyond them is eternity.

We listen to God well when we don't just hear his word, but obey it—including controlling our speech, caring for the needy, and showing love, not favouritism.

Genuine, saving faith is seen in our actions, because it produces obedient, loving deeds. We need to beware of counterfeit faith, which does not save.

⊕ talkabout

1. "Sticks and stones may break my bones, but words will never hurt me." How true is that statement, would you say?

⊥ investigate

▶ **Read James 3 v 1-12**

2. Why should Christians think seriously about whether or not they should be gospel teachers (v 1-2)?

DICTIONARY

In check (v 2): under control.

3.   How do verses 3-4 picture the power of our tongues?

• How do verses 5-6 explain the destructiveness of our tongues?

4.   So our tongues are powerful, and destructive. Why is being determined to "tame our tongues" not a solution, according to James (v 7-8)?

5.   What two things do we do with our tongues? Why are they contradictory (v 9-10)?

• Our tongues are the overflow of our hearts. So what is James saying in verses 11-12 about our hearts?

⊡ explore more

optional

> **▶ Read Psalm 12**

How is King David experiencing the kind of cursing that James talks of (v 2-4)?
Who else does David listen to (v 5)?
What is different about God's words (v 6)?
Whose words have most influence over you—those around you (whether friends or people who speak like those in v 2-4), or the Lord*? Why?*

⊖ apply

6. Why do some people find it hard to accept James' diagnosis in these verses, do you think?

• How have you seen in your own life, or around you, tongues being used for great good, and for great destructiveness?

⬇ investigate

If the tongue is beyond our control, how can it ever be possible for us to "keep a tight reign" on it (1 v 26)? The answer lies in what James says next. Our tongues need to be set alight from a different source, and not from "hell" (2 v 6).

❯ **Read James 3 v 13-18**

7. What two sources of wisdom does James point to?

• What does each lead to?

8. Why would verses 17-18 only be possible for someone who has a tight reign on their tongue?

There is a wonderful illustration of what James is saying here in the book of Acts, on the Day of Pentecost, when the Holy Spirit was poured out on the early Christian believers.

❯ **Read Acts 2 v 1-11**

9. Where was this fire from?

10. What did it prompt these Christians to do (v 4, 11, see also v 14-22)?

⊡ apply

11. What is one mark of someone who is truly wise?

12. How can you encourage each other in how you use your tongues?
- In what you do say:

- In what you don't say.

In what ways do you speak a foreign language?

What do you need to pray specifically about when it comes to your use of your tongue, as you ask God for the wisdom to give glory to him, rather than cursing or criticising others?

⬆ pray

Thank God for...

Confess...

Ask for help with...

5 James 4 v 1-12
HOW TO COME BACK TO GOD

The story so far

We need to ask for wisdom to know joy and resist temptation in trials, knowing they mature us; and we must not only listen to God's word, but obey it.

Genuine, saving faith is seen in our actions, because it produces obedient, loving deeds. We need to beware of counterfeit faith, which does not save.

Our tongues are naturally both powerful and destructive; we need to seek God's wisdom so that our words are guided by the Spirit and bring glory to Christ.

⊕ talkabout

1. What, or who, causes fights and quarrels:
    * in the workplace or the home?

    * in church?

    * Why are churches so often undermined or split by conflicts, do you think?

⊕ investigate

Question One is the same question James poses in verse 1 of this passage.

❯ Read James 4 v 1-5

2. When we are involved in a quarrel, our instinct is to see the other person as the cause of the fight! But where does James locate the problem (v 1-2)?

> **DICTIONARY**
>
> **Covet (v 2):** long to possess what someone else has; envy.
> **Enmity (v 4):** being an enemy.

3. When Christians act on their selfish desires, what are they forgetting (end v 2)?

• What else should Christians remember (v 3)?

4. How might praying, and praying according to God's priorities and not theirs, change the way James' readers see their own desires, and their church conflicts?

So it is our selfish hearts that lead to conflict with each other. To put it another way, conflict shows that we have selfish hearts.

5. What else does it show about us (v 4)? How do the words James chooses to use in verse 4 show us the seriousness of sin?

➔ **apply**

6. In what ways are you (as a church and individually) most tempted to try to be friends with God *and* the world?

7. How does thinking of sin as "spiritual adultery" change our view of:
• ourselves?

• our sins?

• our temptations?

⊡ getting personal

Think of a sin you fall prey to on a regular basis. What would be different if, next time you are tempted, you remember that you are being tempted to commit spiritual adultery?

How will you make sure you see that sin in this way?

⊙ investigate

▶ **Read James 4 v 6-12**

8. What truths about God does verse 6 contain? Why is this amazing, considering the truth about us in verse 4?

⊡ explore more

optional

▶ **Read Hosea 1 v 2-3; 3 v 1-6**

Why is the prophet Hosea told to marry his wife, Gomer (1 v 2-3)? Why is Hosea told to restore his relationship with his wife (3 v 1)? What does it cost him (v 2)? Since Hosea is a picture of God, what are we meant to understand about his relationship with his people? How is Hosea's marriage a powerful picture for us today about who we are and who God is? How does it move us to love God instead of the world?

In verses 7-10, James shows us what it means to approach God humbly, able to receive his grace, by telling us what genuine repentance looks like.

9. Trace out the stages of genuine repentance that James lays out (v 7-9).

• How does the promise of verse 10 encourage us to genuinely repent?

It was conflict in the church (v 1-3) that showed that these Christians' hearts were adulterous.

10. What does James say will be an outward sign that shows these Christians have really repented (v 11)?

⊕ apply

11. How similar, or different, is your usual view of repentance to James' explanation of real repentance here? Which parts of genuine repentance do you find it easiest to forget or underplay, and why?

⊡ getting personal

"He gives us more grace" (v 6). How fully do you appreciate God's grace to you?

"Humble yourselves ... and he will lift you up" (v 10). How can you make sure that deliberate, humble repentance is part of your daily routine?

12. How will our Christian lives be damaged, possibly fatally, if we forget to live out any one of these verses?

• v 4

• v 6

• v 7-9

• How can you as a church help one another to believe and live by the truths and commands of these verses?

⬆ **pray**

Use verse 4 to confess your sinfulness to God. If you're willing to, then name specific sins out loud (see James 5 v 16a).

Use verses 7-9 to genuinely repent of your sins.

Then use verses 6 and 10 to praise God for his forgiveness and grace.

6 James 4 v 13 – 5 v 20
WISDOM IN PLANNING, PATIENCE IN SUFFERING

The story so far

We need to ask for wisdom to know joy and resist temptation in trials, knowing they mature us; and we must not only listen to God's word, but obey it.

Genuine, saving faith is seen in our actions. And it is seen in the way we speak—no longer destructively, but guided by the Spirit and glorifying Jesus.

We are spiritually adulterous towards God—and so we are called to genuinely repent. Wonderfully, when we do, God continues to give us more grace.

⊕ talkabout

1. What does the way in which someone plans their schedule reveal about them spiritually, would you say?

   • What about the way in which someone responds to suffering?

⊕ investigate

▶ **Read James 4 v 13-17**

2. Who is James speaking to in these verses (v 13)? What does their priority appear to be?

3. In verse 14, what does James want to remind the verse-13 people about:
  • the future?

  • themselves?

4. What should they say instead?

5. How does verse 15 help us to see why verse 13 is, as James puts it, "arrogant", "boasting" and "evil" (v 16)?

⤷ apply

6. Why is it good news that God is in charge of the future?

⊎ investigate

7. How should these verses affect both how we plan, and what we plan?

We are not to reject planning, nor are we to demonise making money. But what we are to do, James says, is to acknowledge the will of God and to allow that to put our lives, plans and priorities in perspective. That is far easier said than done—but done it must be.

⊡ getting personal

When you next plan something, how will you remember that God is in charge, and you are not?

When you next plan something, how will you make sure you're being guided by God's priorities, and not those of your bank balance?

⊎ investigate

❯ Read James 5 v 1-12

8. Who is James speaking to in verses 1-6?

> **DICTIONARY**
>
> **Testify (v 3):** witness.
> **Yield (v 7):** give; produce.
> **Swear (v 12):** make an oath.

• And what does he warn them about?

9. Why should Christians be "patient and stand firm" when they suffer or are exploited (v 7-9)?

10. What examples does James point us to, and what point is he making with each?

• v 7

• v 10-11a

• v 11b

⊡ **explore more**

optional

▶ **Read James 5 v 13-18**

How should Christians respond to:
• trouble?   • happiness?   • sickness?
How does Elijah's example encourage us to do this (v 16b-18)?

→ apply

❯ Read James 5 v 19-20

In these verses, James tells us that as "brothers and sisters" we have the responsibility to seek to "bring ... back" someone who is wandering from the life of genuine faith.

DICTIONARY

Elders (v 14): leaders.
Anoint (v 14): smear; rub.
Multitude (v 20): large number.

11. How might you spot "wandering" when it comes to scheduling and suffering?

- How committed are you to bringing people back? What would that look like?

⊡ getting personal

If a Christian you know is wandering in some way, it is your responsibility to call them back. It needs to be done carefully, prayerfully and lovingly—but it does need to be done. It may save someone's life.

Are you willing to take the risk and put in the effort?

Is there someone who you need to pray for, and speak to, *today*?

12. Think back through the whole of the letter of James. What has he shown you a life of genuine faith looks like? What have you, as a group, found most challenging?

⬆ **pray**

Use your answers to Questions Eleven and Twelve to prompt your prayers, and then finish by praising God for all that you have because of your faith in "our glorious Lord Jesus Christ" (2 v 1).

Genuine faith
LEADER'S GUIDE

Leader's Guide

INTRODUCTION

Leading a Bible study can be a bit like herding cats—everyone has a different idea of what the passage could be about, and a different line of enquiry that they want to pursue. But a good group leader is more than someone who just referees this kind of discussion. You will want to:

- correctly understand and handle the Bible passage. But also...

- encourage and train the people in your group to do this for themselves. Don't fall into the trap of spoon-feeding people by simply passing on the information in the Leader's Guide. Then...

- make sure that no Bible study is finished without everyone knowing how the passage is relevant for them. What changes do you all need to make in the light of the things you have been learning? And finally...

- encourage the group to turn all that has been learned and discussed into prayer.

Your Bible-study group is unique, and you are likely to know better than anyone the capabilities, backgrounds and circumstances of the people you are leading. That's why we've designed these guides with a number of optional features. If they're a quiet bunch, you might want to spend longer on *talkabout*. If your time is limited, you can choose to skip *explore more*, or get people to look at these questions at home. Can't get enough of Bible study? Well, some studies have optional extra homework projects. As leader, you can adapt and select the material to the needs of your particular group.

So what's in the Leader's Guide? The main thing that this Leader's Guide will help you to do is to understand the major teaching points in the passage you are studying, and how to apply them. As well as guidance for the questions, the Leader's Guide for each session contains the following important sections:

THE BIG IDEA

One or two key sentences will give you the main point of the session. This is what you should be aiming to have fixed in people's minds as they leave the Bible study. And it's the point you need to head back toward when the discussion goes off at a tangent.

SUMMARY

An overview of the passage, including plenty of useful historical background information.

OPTIONAL EXTRA

Usually this is an introductory activity that ties in with the main theme of the Bible study, and is designed to "break the ice" at the beginning of a session. Or it may be a "homework project" that people can tackle during the week.

So let's take a look at the various different features of a Good Book Guide:

⊕ talkabout

Each session kicks off with a discussion question, based on the group's opinions or experiences. It's designed to get people talking and thinking in a general way about the main subject of the Bible study.

⬇ investigate

The first thing you and your group need to know is what the Bible passage is about, which is the purpose of these questions. But watch out—people may come up with answers based on their experiences or teaching they have heard in the past, without referring to the passage at all. It's amazing how often we can get through a Bible study without actually looking at the Bible! If you're stuck for an answer, the Leader's Guide contains guidance for questions. These are the answers to direct your group to. This information isn't meant to be read out to people—ideally, you want them to discover these answers from the Bible for themselves. Sometimes there are optional follow-up questions (see ☑ in guidance for questions) to help you help your group get to the answer.

🔀 explore more

These questions generally point people to other relevant parts of the Bible. They are useful for helping your group to see how the passage fits into the "big picture" of the whole Bible. These sections are OPTIONAL—only use them if you have time. Remember that it's better to finish in good time having really grasped one big thing from the passage, than to try and cram everything in.

➔ apply

We want to encourage you to spend more time working at application—too often, it is simply tacked on at the end. In the Good Book Guides, apply sections are mixed in with the investigate sections of the study. We hope that people will realise that application is not just an optional extra, but rather, the whole purpose of studying the

Bible. We do Bible study so that our lives can be changed by what we hear from God's word. If you skip the application, the Bible study hasn't achieved its purpose.

These questions draw out practical lessons that we can all learn from the Bible passage. You can review what has been learned so far, and think about practical differences that this should make in our churches and our lives. The group gets the opportunity to talk about what they personally have learned.

💬 getting personal

These can be done at home, but it is well worth allowing a few moments of quiet reflection during the study for each person to think and pray about specific changes they need to make in their own lives. Why not have a time for reporting back at the beginning of the following session, so that everyone can be encouraged and challenged by one another to make application a priority?

⬆ pray

In Acts 4 v 25-30 the first Christians quoted Psalm 2 as they prayed in response to the persecution of the apostles by the Jewish religious leaders. Today however, it's not as common for Christians to base prayers on the truths of God's word as it once was. As a result, our prayers tend to be weak, superficial and self-centred rather than bold, visionary and God-centred.

The prayer section is based on what has been learned from the Bible passage. How different our prayer times would be if we were genuinely responding to what God has said to us through his word.

1

James 1 v 1-18
JOY IN TRIALS

THE BIG IDEA

Christians can know joy and resist temptation in trials because we know that beyond the trials lies eternal life, and that God works in our trials to mature us as believers. We need to ask wholeheartedly for God's wisdom to see our trials in this way.

SUMMARY

In this opening section of James' letter, he encourages believers to keep going in faith and love through all the difficulties of this life, to the day when, "having stood the test, that person will receive the crown of life that the Lord has promised" (v 12). How can we do this? By viewing our trials, whatever they are, as "pure joy", because we know what lies beyond them, and that trials produce perseverance, and that as we persevere, we become more and more "mature" in our faith (v 2-4). James knows this is not how we naturally view trials—so he tells us to do three things:

- Ask God for wisdom—and do so wholeheartedly, not hedging our bets and praying while also seeing if the world has something better on offer (v 5-8).
- Remember and find our confidence in our spiritual position. If we are poor, we need to remember that we are loved and blessed; if rich, that we are sinners whose wealth is fleeting, and who need grace (v 9-11).
- Understand where temptation comes from and where it leads, since temptations are often prompted by trials (v 13-15).

As you will see in this study, if and as we learn to do these things, we will find ourselves responding to hard times in a very different way from how the world does, and we naturally would: with a "pure joy" that only the gospel enables.

OPTIONAL EXTRA

Find some (appropriate) questions sent into an agony aunt. Read each out and ask your group to guess the answer given, before revealing it. Make up two final questions that are about facing periods of suffering—perhaps health, or job, or relationally. For each answer, simply say: "Think of this time with joy". Ask your group for their reactions to that advice. This will draw out the surprising, counterintuitive and challenging nature of the advice James gives in 1 v 2.

GUIDANCE FOR QUESTIONS

1. What do you see as the relationship between joy and suffering? Instinctively, we see them as opposed to one another—the more we suffer, the less joyful we will feel. In order to be joyful, we need to end the struggle. **Why?** First, areas of suffering very easily become all-consuming—it becomes hard to think about anything else, and so other aspects of life which are joyful pale into insignificance. Second, suffering is the removal of something that we want to have—health, a relationship, financial security, etc. We tend to see our joy, or happiness, as relying on having a certain amount/level of certain things—if one of those is removed, then we will not be joyful.

- **How do wealth and poverty usually influence our joy? Why?** Wealth tends to be a source of joy, or at least to enable us to feel joyful about other parts of our life. So we tend to view poverty (even relative poverty) as removing a sense of wellbeing. To be poor is usually seen as being something of a failure in life.

2. How does James' description of himself and of his readers make reading this letter exciting? James is "a servant of God and of the Lord Jesus Christ" (v 1). So the letter is written by a first-generation church leader to whom the risen Jesus had appeared (1 Corinthians 15 v 7), and who led the church in Jerusalem (e.g. Acts 21 v 17-19). We are listening to a man who knew Jesus.

And the letter is to "the twelve tribes scattered among the nations" (James 1 v 1). The "twelve tribes" was a way of describing Israel—and the Jews had been scattered throughout the Roman world. So James is writing to Jewish Christians outside of Israel, who live scattered among those who do not know the God of the Bible. So this is exciting for us to read—we may or may not be Jewish, but we too are God's people scattered among the nations.

⊗

• **James was actually Jesus' biological brother. In light of this, what is striking about how he describes himself in James 1 v 1? What does this suggest is most important to him?** More important than James' biological connection with Jesus is the spiritual one he enjoys. James sees himself as a servant before he sees himself as a human family member.

3. What kind of person does James want his readers to be, does verse 12 suggest? Believers who keep going through hard times with their faith in and love for Christ intact (or even increased), and

therefore who receive wonderful blessing from God at the end of it all.

4. What is the main way we can be or become this type of person (v 2)? By considering whatever trials that come our way as "pure joy".

Notice James says, "Consider". He is not telling us so much how to feel as how to think. He is not saying, *Pretend this is fun.* Nor is he calling us always to have a sickly grin or stiff upper lip. No, James is telling us to think about our trials in a certain way. There is a point of view we need to adopt, a particular way to consider what is going on. Notice that James says "whenever"—trials should not be unexpected, for they are part and parcel of the regular Christian life. And notice that James talks of trials of "many kinds". What he is about to say applies to us all—to the trial that we are facing, not just those that others are facing. James is saying that there is a way to think about times of suffering that will bring us joy.

• **How is this view different from how we tend to view suffering?** This relates back to Q1. We tend to view trials as times that prompt sadness, despair, bitterness or anger. At best, we grit our teeth and aim to get through them.

• **What reasons does James give for viewing suffering in this way (v 3-4)?** Trials teach us to persevere (v 3). They put us in situations where it is not easy to keep going, and where we will only do so with a measure of determination. And perseverance is the means to a wonderful end: that we be "mature and complete, not lacking anything" (v 4). James is talking about being rounded and formed as a Christian, growing into the very people we were created and saved to be. This is actually what we most long for as Christians (or at least what we should most long for): to become more whole in Christ; to know him more fully and intimately. And it is trials that give us this opportunity to mature in our faith. In fact, we can't get there without trials. They are the spiritual equivalent of growbags. It is how the Christian life works; faith grows through learning to persevere in hardship. Suffering proves, strengthens and deepens our faith. Faith is a little like a muscle in the human body. It is as it is worked out that it grows. It needs something to push against. Physical training is a painful and sweaty process. Muscle growth requires discomfort. Faith needs the pushback of trials for us to grow spiritually. Trials and difficulties are an opportunity to cling on to the promises of God more tightly. God is not after just a little bit of change in our lives. So if all we pursue is comfort, we will never become truly mature in our faith.

5. What should we do if we struggle to have the "wisdom" to look at our trials in this way (v 5)? We "should ask God" for that wisdom. We don't need to feel in the middle of trials that this is a time when we have to prove ourselves—to show God that we've been paying attention in class and now have it all figured out. It is OK to need guidance. And we need to ask for it.

- **How will God respond (v 5)?** When we ask for wisdom, he "gives [it] generously". God is not tightfisted with his wisdom. And he responds in this way to "all" who ask. God's wisdom is not something that is restricted to only a few privileged Christians. God intends it to be enjoyed and used by all his people. Not only this, but he gives to all "without finding fault". When we come to our Father asking for

wisdom in the middle of great turmoil, he is not shaking his head saying, *You really messed all that up... Come on, don't you know by now how to handle this?* He is not tut-tutting as he guides and leads us.

- **What warning does James give in verses 6-8?** We must "believe and not doubt" as we ask for wisdom (v 6), otherwise we cannot "expect to receive anything from the Lord" (v 7), and we will then be "unstable" in our faith and in our life (v 8). **How does "double-minded" (v 8) help us to understand what he means by "doubt" in verse 6?** At first glance, these verses may leave us reeling. Most if not all Christians experience doubt at some point. Does this mean we then cannot expect God to give us the wisdom of his perspective on trials? No—by "doubt", James means someone who is "double-minded" (v 8); someone we might think of as fickle, or two-faced. In other words, the doubter is someone who wants to hedge their bets. They'll ask God for wisdom, but they'll also look over their shoulder to see if anyone has anything better on offer. They'll check out what the Bible says, but they'll also check out what the wisdom of the world says. They don't believe God's ways will necessarily and always be the best ways. They are double-minded: trying to live in more than one direction at once. They think they can switch between worldly wisdom and God's wisdom at will and get the best of both.

EXPLORE MORE
Read Romans 5 v 1-8 ... What do we enjoy as a result of this [i.e. being justified by faith] (v 1-2)?
"Peace with God" (v 1)—this is not an inner sense, but an actual reality. We who were enemies of God because of sin have now

been declared to be at peace with him. *Access to God (v 2)*—we can speak to God any time we want to, knowing that because of his grace we can stand in his presence. *Certain hope of being in glory (end v 2)*— "boast" here means to "have confidence in"; a Christian knows for certain that they will one day be in God's glorious presence.

What else do we do, and why (v 3-4)? "Glory in our sufferings"—or, as NIV84 puts it, "rejoice in our sufferings". We do this because we know that suffering produces perseverance (i.e. "testedness"); which produces "character" (Christ-likeness); which leads to our "hope" growing—that is, our confidence in and excitement about our glorious future (v 2). So we don't rejoice about suffering, but we do rejoice at what is happening in our suffering, and we find ourselves rejoicing about our future beyond our suffering.

How does Paul reassure us this isn't just wishful thinking in:

• **v 5?** The Holy Spirit has brought God's love into our hearts. We have experienced God and his love, and this confirms it is not just wishful thinking.

• **v 6-8?** Even more than this, we can look back at God sending his Son to die for us, and know that God loves us and that we are justified.

How do Paul's words here reinforce and add to James' message in James 1 v 1-8? Your group will have spotted the links as they answered the previous questions. Suffering is to be met by joy because we know where we are heading, and we know what suffering produces in us: in Romans 5, greater hope; in James 1, greater maturity.

6. APPLY: How should knowing what Christians will receive in the future (v 12) affect our view of suffering now? What stops us viewing our lives

like this? We know that the suffering will not last, and will not have the final word. One day, if we keep going in faith, we will receive a "crown of life". The only thing weighing us down will be the crown we have been given by God. There is a wonderful, eternal life in store for us beyond our suffering—so we should not be totally consumed by the suffering or think/act as though life is over, or can never be joyful. We struggle to view life like this when we forget: that there is eternal life ahead; that it is wonderful; that our place there has already been promised by Christ. It is hard to view life like this when we are surrounded by friends, family and/or work colleagues who have a very different perspective, because they are living for this life, not the next one.

7. APPLY: What is attractive about being able to consider trials with "pure joy"? How wonderful to actually have a deep joy that is unaffected both by the highs and the lows of life—to have a type of happiness that cannot be snatched away if we lose our health, or are bereaved, or face uncertainty in our work, and so on. It is not easy to consider our trials with "pure joy", but it is wonderful to be able to do so.

• **How is this a strong witness to those around us?** It is in suffering that we, and others, are able to see what is most important to us. When something good is taken from us, if our joy rests in knowing Christ and looking forward to eternal life, we will be very different from non-Christians, who would be despairing or angry that they had lost this good thing. We need to remember that trials are an opportunity to show how wonderful it is to know that we have all we need in Jesus—that we can lose other things we love, and still be joyful even as we struggle.

8. How should humble (poor) Christians view themselves (v 9-11)? And rich ones? How does the world view these two states differently? Whichever end of the pecking order we may happen to be at, James' advice is the same: we are to boast in our position. Not in our financial position, but our spiritual position—the position we have before God: the position in which the gospel of Jesus Christ has placed us.

So the poor should "take pride in their high position" (v 9). In Christ, they are a somebody. However materially lacking life might be, there is an incredible inheritance to look forward to. The world may see the poor as unfortunate, or failures; they may themselves be tempted towards bitterness—but, as Christians, they should see themselves in the light of the gospel. Spiritually, they have everything.

On the other hand, the rich should "take pride in their humiliation" (v 10). They have had to acknowledge before God that however materially rich they are, they are utterly bankrupt spiritually. Spiritually, they are a charity case. So while the world tends to define the rich by their wealth and look up to the wealthy, the gospel again contradicts the assessment of the world.

• **Why does the gospel encourage the poor, and humble the rich?** This question draws out the gospel truths that exalt and encourage the poor, and humble the wealthy. The gospel tells someone who is poor that they are unimaginably loved by and valuable to God, and that they have unfathomable riches in eternity. And the gospel tells someone who is rich that their wealth cannot be taken through death, and will mean nothing when they

stand before God. They need his grace, which their money cannot buy.

9. Where does temptation not come from? It does not come from God (v 13). We find it very easy to blame God for the temptations we experience, e.g. *God is the one who made me like this… He's the one who put me in this situation.*

But James counters this by reminding us of what God is like: "God cannot be tempted by evil". He is untemptable. Sin holds no attraction for him, as it does for us. He is utterly pure. And because of this, we can be sure that he is not trying to trip us up, looking for ever more inventive ways to tempt us into sin. **Where does it come from (v 13-14)?** Temptation comes from our "own evil desire" (v 14). The uncomfortable truth is this: the evil desire tugging away at us is our own. We can't blame any of the things around us. It is not the fault of our parents, our peers, our circumstances, our genes or our God. The desire to sin comes from our own hearts.

• **Where does temptation lead, if it is not resisted (v 15)?** James describes the process in terms of two births. Desire gives birth to sin. Our desires, when fed and nurtured in our hearts and minds, inevitably lead to action. When those desires are ungodly, so too is the resulting behaviour. Sin is born. And once born, it does what babies do—it grows stronger. And then sin gives birth to death (v 15—see Romans 6 v 23). As sinners, who have listened to our evil desires and so have given in to temptation, we face death, both physical and spiritual.

10. Temptation does not come from God. What *does* come from him (v 17-18)? Everything we have that is good.

Remember that James is still helping his readers deal with trials and face them with joy. And in times of trial, we tend to lose sight of the good things God has given us. And the most wonderful gift God has given us as believers is new birth (v 18). Sin gives birth to death; God has given us a very different birth, into new life.

☒

- **What do verses 17-18 tell us about:**
  - **God?** He is sovereign—Father of the heavenly lights, Creator of everything.
    - He is dependable—he does not change. Everything else changes—like shadows, always shifting—but God is unchanging and constant. So we can trust his promises and be confident in his commitment to us.
    - He is gracious—he has given us so many good things—most of all new "birth through the word of truth".
  - **conversion?**
    - Its origin: It has been given to us. It comes as a gracious gift from God. He "chose" to give it; we didn't earn it.
    - Its means: This new birth has come by the "word of truth". The births of sin and death came as a result of our listening to our evil desires; this has come through our coming under the word of God. So powerful is the message of Jesus that it can make us into new people.
    - Its result: We become "firstfruits" of God's creation. The firstfruits are the initial batch of a farmer's crop that guarantees the rest of the harvest is on its way. Our new life is the beginning of what God is up to, a plan that incorporates the whole of creation.

11. APPLY: What are the particular

temptations we might face when we feel we are: These will vary from person to person, and (to a certain extent) context to context—allow your group to give different answers. But here are some suggestions:
- **in a period of great trial?** We may be tempted to think God does not love us; to disobey God in order to end the trial; to forget about eternity and despair or grow bitter; to envy others.
- **poor?** Again, there will be great temptation to envy, bitterness, and stealing (see Proverbs 30 v 8-9 for this, and for the "trial" of being rich).
- **rich?** There may be a temptation towards pride, self-reliance, idolising possessions, or indifference to others' suffering.

12. APPLY: What thought process have verses 13-18 taught us to go through, and encourage others to go through, when temptation comes?
- This is not God's doing; I can't excuse myself for how I deal with this temptation.
- I am being tempted by this because my heart has wrong desires. They are wanting to drag me away from obedience.
- What I am being tempted to do is a sin. It matters.
- If I give in, I am not getting this sin out of my system; I am allowing it to grow more powerful, and harder to resist next time.
- Sin leads to death. There is a place called hell and, without Christ's sin-bearing death, my sin is what takes me there.
- At this moment, I am at risk of being deceived into forgetting what temptation is and why I'm being tempted, and what sin leads to.
- So I will resist this temptation, and instead I will enjoy knowing God, enjoying his good gifts, and remembering that I have new life from him.

2 James 1 v 19 – 2 v 13
LISTEN WELL

THE BIG IDEA

We listen to God rightly when we don't just hear his word, but obey it. This obedience brings freedom, and involves controlling our speech, caring for the vulnerable, and not displaying worldly favouritism.

SUMMARY

Every time we open the Bible, it matters that we listen well. Fundamental to what we know about God is that he speaks. It is not an incidental activity. He created the universe by his words (Hebrews 11 v 3, ESV), and, as we have just seen in James, it is how he has chosen to give us new birth, "through the word of truth" (James 1 v 18).

We therefore need to be people who listen properly to what God says. It is another of the areas where James is showing us we can be easily deceived: "Do not merely listen to the word, and so deceive yourselves. Do what it says" (v 22). The danger is that we can think we're responding in the right way to God's word when, in fact, we are not.

So how do we listen properly to God? In a nutshell, to listen to God rightly we need not only to hear his word, but also to accept it and obey it. As we do this, James tells us we will enjoy the freedom and fulfilment that come from living the way we were designed to (v 25). And it will mean that we live in a way that "God our Father accepts" (v 27); the proof that we are listening well to God's word is seen in the presence of certain "determinations" in our lives—we will be careful in how we speak (v 26); we will be caring for the needy (v 27); and we will be keen to keep God's law at every point,

including by not showing favouritism in a worldly way, but rather loving our neighbour in a Christ-like way (2 v 1-7).

Note: This study takes in two crucial sections of James' letter (1 v 19-27 and 2 v 1-13)—you might like to split it into two and take a little longer on each.

OPTIONAL EXTRA

Set up a basic "obstacle course" around the room. Then blindfold a member of your group, and ask them to choose another member to guide them round the obstacles. That second member can speak to, but not touch, the blindfolded member. The point is that it is not sufficient for the member who cannot see simply to hear or listen hard to the instructions given—they need to obey them. If you want to make the challenge harder, allow the rest of the group to give unhelpful instructions to the blindfolded member!

GUIDANCE FOR QUESTIONS

1. What makes someone a good listener? You could return to this question after Q3, or at the end of the study, to see how James answers this question. But at this stage, there are no "wrong answers".

2. What does James say stops someone from being a "good listener" (v 19, 22)? *Verse 19:* Being quicker to speak, and quicker to be angry, than we are to listen—so that we don't listen at all. When our listening slows, it is not only our speech that quickens, but also our annoyance or anger. James is (as the context shows) not only or primarily talking about listening to others, but listening to God in his word.

Note: It is not wrong to be angry—Jesus was angry (e.g. Mark 11 v 15-17). But we can easily be angry at the wrong things in the wrong way; our anger can be quick, misdirected, and selfish. We should ask ourselves, "How quickly have I become angry? What has caused it? On whose behalf am I moved to this anger?"

Verse 22: Listening, but then not doing. Listening is vital, but merely listening is just as bad as not listening at all.

- **What do we do if we listen well to God's word (v 21)?**
  - We get rid of "moral filth" and "evil"—we reject what God does not like.
  - We "humbly accept" the word—we are not passive, merely reading his word and then getting on with our day, but we actively seek to accept and change according to that word.

3. How does the illustration James uses show us the difference between bad listening and good listening (v 23-24)? James imagines someone who looks in a mirror, "goes away and immediately forgets what he looks like" (v 24). We use mirrors to show us a problem so we can sort it out. If the mirror shows us something is wrong or embarrassing, we sort it out, immediately! James' point is that God's word is to have the same effect on us as a mirror. We are supposed to act on what it shows us. Bad listening is to listen, but then to forget instead of act. Good listening involves acting on what we have heard (or read).

4. How does verse 25 motivate us to listen well to God's word? If we obey God's word—if we do it as well as hear it—we will be blessed, as we enjoy the freedom it gives. Notice this person is "blessed in

what they do"—now, rather than just in eternity.

If we want to enjoy real freedom, we'll need to obey God's law. Freedom is not the removal of all constraint (a fish is free to jump out of the water, but it will not bring the fish freedom!). Freedom is found by living in the environment we were designed to flourish in. And humanity was designed to live according to God's law. So obedience (strange as it sounds to western ears) is what makes us free. Life is never better without God's word, and never poorer with it.

- **How is God's word described in verse 25? How does this teach us how we should respond to all of God's word—whether it's history, or poetry, or a letter, and so on?** As "law". There are many different kinds of writing in the Bible. Many parts take the form of direct commands that need to be obeyed. Other parts are narrative, poetry, song, etc. But by referring to God's word in general as "law", James is reminding us that all of it is calling us to do something—all of it demands a response of repentance and faith. It is good to ask of any passage, "How should this affect my thinking? My attitude? My behaviour?"

5. What is the kind of "religion" that pleases God (v 26-27)?
- *Controlled speech (v 26):* Not controlling our speech is a sign that we are not actually following God. James expects that Christians will have, and will pursue, a measure of control over what they say. (Note: James gives much more detail on this issue in 3 v 1-12—see Study Four.)
- *Determination to care for the needy (v 27):* The orphan and widow in James' day were

the most destitute and vulnerable. James says the true Christian will have a concern to help and provide for those who need it. The distress of the vulnerable will matter to us.

* *Resolve to avoid the moral pollution of the world (v 27):* There are many ways the world's cultures pull in an opposite direction to the way God calls us to live, and the Christian is to obey God by rejecting them. But James probably is still referring to a determination to value and care for the needy rather than prioritise the rich and influential, which is a theme he will pick up on immediately in 2 v 1-7 (see Q8-12). So the "pollution" James has in mind is primarily economic indifference.

* **How does this add to our understanding of what a "good listener" is when it comes to God's word?** A good listener will be the person whose "religion" matches this description in v 26-27—controlled speech, care for the needy, and rejection of the world's ways when they're in opposition to God's.

6. APPLY: Why is it very easy to listen to the word wrongly? Let your group share their insights. Some possibilities:

* It is easy to think that understanding means we have listened. And it is much easier for our lives if we never actually have to change.

* We can be, rightly, very concerned to understand a passage properly in its biblical context, etc. But we can be so busy doing this that we fail to think about how it applies to us.

* When hearing preaching, if the suggested applications don't apply to us, we can fail to do the hard work of working out how the passage does apply to our situation.

* It is also easy to work out how the word applies to others, rather than to ourselves. **What ways have you found to keep yourself listening well?** Again, let the group share insights. Make sure the conversation is practically focused. In general, though, it's helpful to think in terms of ensuring we:

* *listen well with others.* Study the Bible regularly in small groups, which exist not only to understand a passage, but to help each other apply it; remind each other of it; and hold one another accountable in our lives.

* *listen well alone.* Set aside a time each day to read the word, and/or to reflect on it. Don't assume your group members are reading their Bibles every day, or even fairly regularly. See page 78-79 for some resources that may help.

7. APPLY: If you had to come up with four or five "items of evidence" that show someone is a committed Christian, would you come up with the ones James does in verses 19, 21, and 27? Why / why not? How we speak, our habits of anger, our determination to fight "moral filth", and our treatment of the vulnerable among and around us are not necessarily high up on most "evidence lists". (We might have: church attendance, Bible knowledge, serving the church, sexual morality, etc. Each church culture has its own particular "list", subconsciously.) Encourage your group to think about why we might have very different evidence to James.

* **How does this challenge us about our own Christian lives?** We may be regulars at church, serving in some ministry, reading our Bibles, faithful to our spouses, good parents, etc.—and yet not be living in a way that God finds "acceptable" if our tongues are loose, and we show little

or no practical compassion to those who need help. This is extremely challenging, particularly to those of us from more conservative churches. We rightly care about sound doctrine, but this must never become an end in itself.

8. What is the command (2 v 1)? Don't show favouritism.

• **Can you put James' example in v 2-3 into the context of your own church?** This will vary, church by church—the important thing is to realise that, while James' scenario may not be repeated in your church, that does not mean you are not in danger of acting out of favouritism. The kind of favouritism James is talking about reflects a particular attitude to people we can all have, and the example he has given us is just one expression of it. Favouritism of the sort James has been describing is letting the world determine how much spiritual worth someone has, based on their economic standing (or any other measure). It is a way of thinking that Christians can slip into all too easily. Churches need to take great care not to think of a wealthy unbeliever as being more important or worthy of ministry than a poor unbeliever, or to make a fuss over someone important and powerful that we would never make over someone who is marginal, or to be far more excited about a celebrity coming into church one day than a homeless person.

9. Why should Christians not show favouritism?

• **v 4:** It puts the one showing favouritism in the position of "judge", deciding who is more and who is less valuable or useful. And it is "evil", because, as we saw in 1 v 27, it contradicts the marks of authentic religion, which is inclined towards the needy, not away from them.

• **v 5:** It goes against the grain of how God works. He has always tended to choose those who are "poor in the eyes of the world". Globally, this is still true. This is not to say that God loves the rich less than he loves the poor, or that the poor somehow deserve the sacrificial death of Jesus more than the rich. But it is to say that God chooses to bless the very people James' readers (then and now) tend to shun.

• **v 6-7:** The rich are causing trouble for this church—and often it's those the world sees as "great" (either in terms of wealth, or intellect, or other measures) who exploit or mock the church.

• **v 8:** To show favouritism is to break the "royal law" (the law King Jesus used as part of his executive summary of the whole law in Mark 12 v 29-31), because it means not loving all our neighbours. (This is Jesus' point in the parable of the Good Samaritan, see Luke 10 v 25-37.) It bears repeating: favouritism breaks God's law.

EXPLORE MORE
Read 1 Corinthians 1 v 26-31. What kind of people did God call in the Corinthian church? Those who were NOT wise or influential or noble—those who were "foolish" and "weak".
What point are both Paul, and James (James 2 v 5), making? That God does not tend to choose those who are impressive in the eyes of the world—and so we should not seek to be impressive (Paul's point in 1 Corinthians) or to seek out and prioritise impressive people (James' point in James 2).
Read Isaiah 52 v 13 – 53 v 10. If we show favouritism to wealthy and impressive people, over poor and unimpressive people, what does that

suggest we have forgotten about our Lord and Saviour? We follow a crucified criminal. "There were many who were appalled at him—his appearance was so disfigured beyond that of any human being" (Isaiah 52 v 14). Would we rush to welcome him into our church? Would we think him "strategic"? Would he look like someone worth watching for future Christian leadership? Favouritism suggests that we have forgotten what kind of man our Saviour was, and how it was he saved us.

10. If a Christian shows favouritism in their treatment of others, how much does it matter whether they're a murderer or adulterer? Why (v 9-11)? Favouritism breaks the law (v 9)—it is sin. And when we break part of the law, we break all of the law (v 10), even if we are keeping every other part of the law. God's law is either all kept, or it is broken. So if I break the law in any place—whether through murder, adultery, or failing to love my neighbour by showing favouritism, I "have become a law-breaker".

11. What does James want his readers to remember as they "speak and act" towards others (v 12-13)? V 12: God's law judges us—it exposes whether or not we have been impacted and shaped by a real faith in Christ. The law that gives freedom as we obey it also judges us if we disobey it. V 13: God will not show mercy to those who are not merciful. Showing mercy to others is a sign of being a true follower of Christ; not showing mercy to those who need it is a sign that we have not really responded to the gospel. This is because mercy defines the gospel: Christ loved us even when we were unlovely and undeserving (Romans 5 v 8). Just as God's mercy saves us from his judgment

(end James 2 v 13), so our grasping of the gospel will mean that our mercy flows more powerfully than our judgment/favouritism. **How would this affect their behaviour in the example James gave in v 2-3?** The poor man would be made just as welcome as the rich man. Both would be treated on the basis of God's law—love your neighbour—and the gospel—show mercy—rather than on the basis of his worldly standing or possible "use" to the church.

12. APPLY: How might you as individuals, in your church, or in wider Christian circles, give priority (i.e. show favouritism) to those the world sees as "strategic"? This will vary from church to church and culture to culture. It might be worth thinking about who the world around you exalts (those who are economically powerful, or from the right family background, or who have "respectable" professions, or are socially well-connected, or are intelligent, etc.)—these are the "types" the church may prioritise. It is also worth asking who your church is best at welcoming and accommodating in its services; which "types" are seen as potential future leaders and encouraged into up-front roles; who is most likely to be invited round for a meal in your houses.

- **How does the gospel both challenge you about, and liberate you from, that attitude?** Your answers here depend on your answers to the previous question—but be sure to discuss not only how the gospel challenges these attitudes, but liberates us from them, freeing us to love as we are loved, and from worldly views of people as "better" or "more useful". It is liberating not to be "disappointed" by a church full of "those who are poor in the eyes of the world" (v 5).

3 James 2 v 14-26
FAITH WORKS

THE BIG IDEA

Real, saving Christian faith is seen in our actions, because it produces obedient, loving deeds. Counterfeit faith speaks of belief, and may know the right doctrine, but makes no actual difference.

SUMMARY

Our claims are not always an accurate reflection of what we really think and believe—but our deeds are. We do not always live what we say we believe—but we do always believe what we live out. That is true for Christians as much as anyone else, and it is James' concern here.

In this study, we'll see James drawing a distinction between real, genuine faith—faith that means we are right with God and are truly saved—and counterfeit, fake faith. The frightening truth is that it is possible to claim and believe you possess genuine saving faith, when in fact you do not.

James gives two examples of fake faith. First, sentimental faith (v 15-17), where our words sound good but our deeds are empty, and show that we don't really mean what we say. Second, credal or doctrinal faith, where we believe the right things but they have no impact on us (v 18-19).

Then James gives two real-life examples of genuine faith. First, Abraham, whose saving faith was shown in what he did, in his willingness to obey God even to the extent of sacrificing his son (Genesis 22 v 1-19); second, Rahab, whose faith in the LORD was seen in her protection of Israel's spies, at great risk to herself (Joshua 2 v 1-21).

In order to understand James here, the crucial thing to is to grasp James 2 v 24: "You see that a person is considered righteous by what they do and not by faith alone". James is talking about how we can see saving faith—and it is not in what we say, or what we claim, but what we do. It is faith alone that saves, but the faith that saves is never alone—it always produces godly deeds.

So the study finishes by seeking to encourage the genuine Christian, but also to challenge those who perhaps are complacent, or even do not actually have genuine faith. Be ready to follow up with anyone who needs further time to consider how God is challenging them through this passage.

Note: Many have struggled to see how James is not contradicting Paul's teaching on faith and salvation. This is dealt with in Q11.

OPTIONAL EXTRA

Play a version of the TV game *Golden Balls* (you can watch it on Youtube). Give two group members something good, and identical, e.g. a piece of cake each. They then each have to decide whether to "split" or "steal". If both split, they keep their piece of cake. If both steal, they lose their piece. If one steals and the other splits, the "stealer" gets both bits. They have one minute to talk to each other about what they will decide to do, then they write down secretly either "split" or "steal", and reveal their decision at the same time. Hopefully, some of your group will be prepared to claim they'll split, and then write "steal" (you may need to be prepared to do this yourself!). Of course, it is the actions, not the words, that count.

GUIDANCE FOR QUESTIONS

1. How can you tell if someone is a Christian? Don't look for "the right answer" at this stage, but do encourage people not to settle for "Because they say they are". You'll return to this question as you answer Q10.

• **How can you know if *you* are a real Christian?**

2. How do James' example and conclusion in verses 15-17 answer his questions in verse 14? James imagines a Christian who "is without clothes and daily food" (v 15). "One of" his readers says to that struggling Christian, "Go in peace; keep warm and well fed" (v 16), but does "nothing about their physical needs". "What good" is that? James asks. Answer: *no* good. Words without corresponding deeds are empty sounds—useless. The words are good, but the lack of action shouts, *I don't really mean this.*
And his conclusion is, "In the same way, faith by itself, if it is not accompanied by action, is dead" (v 17).
So verse 14 posed the question of whether a faith that has no accompanying deeds is any "good"—i.e. whether it can "save" that person. And James' answer is "no"—such "faith" is a dead faith (v 17). The words are good, but the lack of action shouts, *I don't really mean this.*
Note: Make clear to your group at this point that James means something specific by the word "faith", which is crucial to remember all the way through this study. "Faith" here means "claiming to trust Christ" (see v 14). The key question is: can such faith—*that is, faith that claims to trust Christ but does not lead to any actions—save someone?*

3. In verses 15-16, what is the difference between what this person suggests with their words, and actually shows by their actions? (You may have answered this question as your answered Q2, but it is so crucial that it is worth underlining.) The person has claimed to care, and to want this "brother or ... sister" to be warm and full. But their actions—or inaction—reveal they do not care at all, and do not much want their fellow church member to be warm and full. Merely wishing someone well in the face of both their need and our ability to help is an indication our spoken sentiments are not sincere. If we have the means to help meet the practical need before us, and choose not to, no amount of nice-sounding words will make up for it.

• **How would someone with genuine faith have responded in this situation?** Bear in mind James 1 v 27. Genuine faith shows itself in genuine actions—here, doing what you can to care for the cold, hungry Christian. So although genuine faith cannot itself be seen, what it produces can.

4. But how does James say real faith reveals itself (v 18)? "By ... deeds." There aren't its-all-in-my-head Christians and my-faith-is-what-I-do Christians. There is genuine faith and there is counterfeit faith; and genuine, saving, get-you-to-heaven faith will always be expressed in how we live. There is no other way to demonstrate it. Faith is seen in deeds.

EXPLORE MORE
Read Mark 2 v 1-12. What does Mark tell us Jesus "saw" (v 5)? "Their faith"—the faith of the men who carried their paralysed friend to meet Jesus.
How did Jesus react to seeing this (v 5)?

He forgave the man's sins (and also, later, healed him, primarily to prove that he had truly forgiven him).

But how was he able to "see" that these men had faith? By what they did—climbing up onto the roof, burrowing through to the room below, and lowering their friend through. Their faith was a physically visible thing, made visible in how they acted.

How does this underline James' teaching about what genuine faith is? True faith can be seen in how someone lives. It is not an invisible way of thinking about God; it is seen in how we behave.

5. What central Christian doctrine does James point to (v 19)? "You believe that there is one God." God is One. It is the cornerstone of a biblical understanding of God: "Hear, O Israel: the Lord our God, the Lord is one" (Deuteronomy 6 v 4). Jesus himself also affirmed the importance of this, quoting this very verse when asked to give his executive summary of the law (Mark 12 v 29). It is the starting point of the ancient church creeds: "We believe in one God…"

Who does he say is in full agreement on this point? The demons. Demons know who God is and they know God is One.

• **What point is he making about "faith" that is only doctrinal—that is, all about believing the right things?** It is no better than the "faith" of demons! If we are tempted to think that having our theology right is what shows we have genuine, saving faith, we need to remember who we share our correct theology with. Profession of faith when no deeds flow from that faith is hot air. Someone saying they believe something is no real indication of whether they really do.

• **What difference does the demons' belief make to them (v 19)? So how is James unfavourably comparing "Christians" whose beliefs make no difference with demons?!** The demons "shudder". They're not unaffected by what they know about God—they know enough of God's greatness to tremble at him. Of course, true Christians will rejoice at the thought of our great God and Father, rather than shuddering and cowering. But James is likely highlighting how the demons are impacted by what they know to be true. How do you know they believe there is one God? They shudder. You can see their belief. It matters to them, and you can see that. And if who God is genuinely matters to "Christians", you will be able to see that, too.

6. APPLY: What kinds of "counterfeit Christianity" is James warning us about in these verses?
1. Wishing someone well while doing nothing to help them, i.e. saying caring things, but not doing anything caring (we could call this "sentimental counterfeit faith")—v 15-17.
2. Affirming something to be true which makes no difference to the way we live (we could call this "doctrinal/creedal counterfeit faith")—v 18-19.

• **Why are these forms of false Christianity easier to live out than genuine Christianity?** Because they don't require us to do anything! It is easy to say something that sounds caring, or to talk about theology and doctrine. It is costly to live differently because we have genuine faith.

• **How can churches allow or even encourage one another to think these counterfeit "Christianities" are genuine, saving faith?** James concern here is that we look at ourselves as individuals and churches, not at the nominalism we might happen to see around us in our culture or in churches "up the road". Think about what your church sees as the "marks" of genuine faith. Is it theological correctness? Or talking lovingly and with concern about struggling Christians? Do you ever challenge each other if/when you see words that may not be matched by actions? Do you assume that someone who says they are a Christian must therefore be a Christian?

7. Read Genesis 15 v 1-6 and 22 v 1-19. What came first—Abraham obeying God in his actions, or Abraham being made righteous (that is, Abraham being saved)? Being made righteous. In Genesis 15, God promised that elderly, childless Abraham would have a son, and countless descendants. Abraham believed God, and this was "credited … to him as righteousness" (v 6). He was made right with God because he believed in the promises of God. It was years later that he proved himself willing to sacrifice that son, Isaac, in Genesis 22.

• **So how were his "faith and his actions … working together" (James 2 v 22) when he proved willing to sacrifice his son? How was the Scripture of Genesis 15 "fulfilled" at that point?** Abraham was willing to obey. And this is why it's significant: it proves Abraham really did trust God. His obedience (seen in Genesis 22) demonstrated the genuineness of faith (seen in Genesis 15). "His faith and his actions were working together"—his actions completed his faith (James 2 v 22). His faith was seen in his obedience. The kind of faith that had been credited to Abraham as righteousness years before in Genesis 15 now produced this act of obedience in Genesis 22—the kind of act only a man of faith would perform; the kind of act that causes the doer to be "considered righteous" (James 2 v 21). The Scripture that had said Abraham believed God was fulfilled—shown to be correct—when Abraham acted out that faith.

• **If Abraham had not had genuine faith, how would he have acted differently in Genesis 22?** He would not have obeyed so radically and trustingly—he would never have been willing to sacrifice his own son, on whom all God's promises rested. Counterfeit faith would have revealed itself in inaction at this point.

8. So how do we see whether or not someone is considered righteous by God (James 2 v 24)? It is easy to skip over the first two words of verse 24, but they are crucial. James is talking about how "you [literally] see" that a person is considered righteous by God, i.e. that they are truly saved. We can tell that someone is righteous by their actions. It is not that their actions make them righteous, but that they reveal that they are righteous—just as Abraham's actions did.

9. Read Joshua 2 v 1-24. How did what Rahab "did" (James 2 v 25) prove that she had genuine faith? The context here is that the people of God are poised to enter the promised land and will need to take the city of Jericho. Spies are dispatched to case the joint before battle is joined. During their reconnaissance they come across Rahab. Word is out that Jewish spies are in the city. The Jericho police are knocking at the door yet Rahab covers for them, sending the police off in the wrong direction and slipping the spies out. These actions align her with the mission of the Israelites, but put her entirely at cross-purposes with her own people. It is incredibly risky. Yet she does it because she has faith in God, as she says in v 9-11. Because she really believes, she acts.

- **If Rahab had not had genuine faith, how would she have acted differently in Joshua 2?** She would never have risked her life by hiding the spies.

10. What do Abraham and Rahab teach us about:

- **the relationship between faith (by which James means the claim to be trusting God) and works?** Again, you may well have covered these two questions in your previous discussions as a group, but they are important to underline. Genuine faith is proved by works, but our works do not save us—as Martin Luther put it, "We are saved by faith alone, but the faith that saves is never alone". Genuine faith is lived-out faith—it is visible and active.

- **how you can know whether or not someone (including you) has genuine faith?** While we do not always live what we say we believe, we do always believe what we live out. So the question is: *are we demonstrating deeds that come from true faith?* If our lifestyle gives no evidence of the faith we claim to have, we need to challenge ourselves as to whether we truly trust in Christ.

11. APPLY: ... How would you explain how Paul and James are not disagreeing

with each other?
1. Paul himself was aware that some believers had misunderstood his teaching, that we are saved by faith alone: "Why not say—as some slanderously claim that we say—'Let us do evil that good may result'?" (Romans 3 v 8). James is not contradicting Paul; rather, he is opposing those who have distorted Paul.
2. James uses the word "faith" in a different way from Paul. For Paul, faith is trusting Christ; we are saved by faith alone, because it is the saving work of Christ alone that we trust. But James has been using "faith" more broadly, describing not just trust in Christ, but the claim to be trusting in Christ. Hence his question at the start of this section about the person who professes faith but has no deeds: "Can *such* faith save them?" (James 2 v 14, my emphasis). Faith here refers to their profession of trust.
3. James is focusing on how we see that a person is truly right with God. And we see it not in what they say (i.e. "I have faith in Jesus"), but by how they live. So Paul is underlining the truth that it is faith in Christ, and nothing more and nothing else, that saves someone. And James is making the point that this kind of genuine, saving faith can be seen in how someone lives—and if it can't be seen, it is probably not genuine faith, whatever someone says or thinks.

12. APPLY: How does this passage challenge complacent Christians? How might it encourage concerned Christians? This passage requires self-examination from all of us. And we respond to challenges like this in quite different ways. Some of us tend to assume we are fine. We have been Christians for a while, we go to church, others think we are Christians— so we are Christians! But James wants complacency to stop—he tells us to look hard at our lives. Are we affected by, and do we live out, what we say is true of us? It could be that some people need to read this passage and rightly conclude that they are not Christians. This is James' aim, after all—to expose false faith. Counterfeit faith does no good and does not save—so to realise we have false faith is vital as it means that we can ask God to give us true, living, saving, action-directing faith.

Equally, some Christians will read these verses and instantly think of their inconsistencies and faults. They might easily find themselves questioning whether they really are Christians at all (and might often worry about this). It is a blessing to have a tender conscience—but the danger is that we so consider our deficiencies that we fail to notice the ways in which we do actually (if imperfectly) express our faith in our actions. We only see the flaws and we easily miss what might be genuine fruit.

With both "types", our self-assessment is superficial. We need to take our time, and we need God's help. We need to pray with David: "But who can discern their own errors? Forgive my hidden faults" (Psalm 19 v 12). We need God to show us where we are truly at, especially if we know we are prone to have a very slanted view of ourselves. One of the means God can use, of course, is Christian people who know us well and who will be honest with us—and we then need to be willing to hear their answer, whether it confirms or corrects what we think.

And if we conclude we have false faith, or are worried that we do, the answer is the same—not to try to do better deeds so that we can have genuine faith, but to look at all Jesus has done and offers us through his life, death and resurrection; and put our trust in him as our Saviour and our Lord, asking God to give us faith. That is genuine faith—and as we enjoy knowing Christ, we'll find our lives being shaped by our faith in him.

James 3 v 1-18

4 TONGUES ON FIRE

THE BIG IDEA
Our tongues are powerful, and they tend to be destructive because they're influenced by hell, not heaven; so we must seek wisdom from above, and learn to speak in ways that are guided by the Spirit.

SUMMARY
In this study, James is focusing on our tongues—their influence, and what they reveal about us. This is a fairly straightforward passage, but it is also very humbling and challenging, as it teaches that:

- our tongues are powerful (v 3-5a).
- our tongues are destructive (v 5-6).
- our tongues have great influence both over the rest of our body, and over many years—one spiteful or unthoughtful sentence can have a huge impact for decades (v 6).
- the reason our tongues are used destructively is because they are influenced by hell—our natural language is the language of Satan (lying, exaggerating, self-serving, malicious, etc—v 6b).
- we cannot help this—humans find it

impossible to tame their tongues (v 7-8).
• our tongues are revealers—they show what our hearts are really like. When our tongues praise God and criticise humans who are made in his image, they show that our hearts aren't godly (v 9-11).

The solution James points us to is not in ourselves and doing better, but in having our tongues "set on fire" by a different source. Verses 13-18 show us two sources of "wisdom", with very different results: earthly wisdom, which causes envy and ambition, disorder and evil, and is "demonic" (v 14-16); and "heavenly wisdom", which shows itself in our deeds, and produces purity, peace, thoughtfulness, mercy and sincerity (v 13, 17-18). James has already shown us how we can have this heavenly wisdom, which will influence our tongues—ask for it (1 v 5).

The end of this study takes your group to Acts 2 v 1-11, to see a different "fire" from the one of James 3 v 6, and a different way of using tongues. The Holy Spirit sets our tongues on fire to praise God and speak of Christ—this is the spoken outworking of having heavenly wisdom. As Christians, our native language has changed, from hellish to heavenly, and from Satan-provoked to God-inspired—we need to learn to speak our new native language more and more fluently, both in what we do say, and what we choose not to say.

OPTIONAL EXTRA

Play a game that demands control over your words. (1) Someone is asked lots of questions, and is never allowed to answer "yes" or "no". (2) Two people talk to one another but are only allowed to talk in questions (so each question must be answered by another question). It is very hard to control your tongue!

GUIDANCE FOR QUESTIONS

1. "Sticks and stones may break my bones, but words will never hurt me." How true is that statement, would you say? There is no right or wrong answer. In some senses, it is true—words cannot inflict physical pain, and we can try to ignore them. However, we do live in a world where words matter. They have the capacity to affect us enormously. The damage done by something said can go far deeper and last much longer than damage done by sticks and stones.

2. Why should Christians think seriously about whether or not they should be gospel teachers (v 1-2)? Teachers will be judged more strictly, because they have the capacity to do particular damage to the church. Their words will either convey the truth, or obscure or even deny it. Therefore, teachers, even more than other Christians, need to keep their tongues in check. In verse 2, James is not describing someone who is never at fault in any way, but someone who generally doesn't stumble in what they say. In other words, James is reiterating the point he made in 1 v 26: a mark of authentic Christian faith is keeping a tight rein on our tongues. Someone who can control their tongue can "keep their whole body in check" (3 v 2). But (as we're about to see), controlling our tongues is not as simple as saying we ought to, or that we want to.

3. How do verses 3-4 picture the power of our tongues? James provides us with two visual aids—horses (v 3) and ships (v 4). The key in each is what actually does the controlling. For horses, a small piece of metal called a bit, which sits in the horse's mouth, can be used by its rider to direct it. That whole animal can be controlled and manipulated by something so small. We see the same idea with ships. Ships are big. Rudders are small—0.1% of a large ship's size. Yet something so comparatively small is able to manoeuvre something so huge.

- **How do verses 5-6 explain the destructiveness of our tongues?** James tells us to "consider" how a destructive forest fire starts (v 5). It can start by just one small spark—and wipe out a whole region. And "the tongue also is a fire" (v 6). Whereas a horse's bit and a ship's rudder can be used positively, a spark that causes a forest fire is always destructive. So, James says, is the tongue.

In verse 6, James provides an anatomy of the tongue, and it is devastating reading:

- It is a "world of evil"—the tongue has a capacity for evil like virtually no other body part.
- "It corrupts the whole body." What we say affects the rest of our body—how we think, feel, act and so on.
- It "sets the whole course of one's life on fire". The tongue is destructive not only throughout our body, but in terms of time, too. Just a few careless words can cause untold damage to us, and to others—careers topple, marriages fall apart, conflicts start, decades of self-loathing are generated, all by what someone uses their tongue to say.
- It "is ... set on fire by hell". Our words are influenced by hell—by which James means that very often, naturally, and usually without us noticing, Satan is using our tongues to do his work.

4. So our tongues are powerful, and destructive. Why is being determined to "tame" our tongues not a solution, according to James (v 7-8)? Because while we can tame wild animals, we do not have the capacity to tame and train our tongues.

It is simply beyond us. If you think your speech is something you can sort out, you are kidding yourself. However successful and able you are, your tongue will never be something you can conquer yourself.

We need to grasp this or we will misunderstand what James is saying in these verses. He is not outlining a programme for mastering our tongues: *Seven Steps to Flawlessly Controlled Speech*. His aim is precisely the opposite. He is saying, *This is not something you are able to do. You need to, desperately: but you can't*. It is beyond human capacity.

5. What two things do we do with our tongues? Why are they contradictory (v 9-10)?
1. We "praise our Lord and Father" (v 9)—we use our tongues well.
2. We "curse human beings, who have been made in God's likeness" (v 9)—we use our tongues for ill.

So "out of the same mouth come praise and cursing" (v 10). Our tongues show how fundamentally inconsistent we are. Notice how James describes the people we criticise or gossip about or speak meanly to—they are "made in God's likeness". We have a capacity to delight in God and then to curse someone that God has not only made, but made in his likeness. We speak in contradictory ways whenever we who sing praise to God on Sunday mornings then speak against someone in some way. James would call it being "double-minded" (1 v 8).

- **Our tongues are the overflow of our hearts. So what is James saying in verses 11-12 about our hearts?** As we look at the world, this principle is very clear: a product is always consistent with its source. Fresh and salt water never flow from the same spring. Fig-trees grow figs,

not olives.
There is no such thing as a blended source that can produce both. What you end up with shows what you started with. So the tongue reveals what is going on underneath—what our hearts are truly like. Our words show what kind of heart we have. In this, James is reflecting what his brother Jesus taught (see Matthew 12 v 33-35). The uncomfortable conclusion is that unChristian speech is evidence of an unchristian heart.

EXPLORE MORE
Read Psalm 12. How is King David experiencing the kind of cursing that James talks of (v 2-4)? David is surrounded by people who are using their tongues to: lie (v 2); flatter with deceitful motives (v 2-3); boast (v 3); be arrogant (v 4); self-servingly exploit others (v 4).
Who else does David listen to (v 5)? The LORD.
What is different about God's words (v 6)? They are "flawless" and "purified". They could not be more valuable. In a world of cheap, flawed words, David knows that there is one Person whose words are never less than perfect, true, and trustworthy—God.
Whose words have most influence over you—those around you (whether friends or people who speak like those in v 2-4), or the LORD? Why?

6. APPLY: Why do some people find it hard to accept James' diagnosis in these verses, do you think? Because it is such a humbling passage. We do not like to be confronted with what our tongues are like (not basically good with a few mistakes now and then); nor do we want to have to think about the destructive effects our words have, or may have had, both on ourselves

and those around us. And it is particularly humbling to hear that we cannot solve the problem ourselves.

• **How have you seen in your own life, or around you, tongues being used for great good, and for great destructiveness?** Give your group a little time to think about this question before you start to share answers; and encourage fairly brief answers. Aim to guide the group towards thinking about their tongues, rather than only other people's tongues. Bear in mind that there may be members who have been very badly hurt by what someone once said to or about them, who continue to carry the scars.

7. What two sources of wisdom does James point to?
1. Verse 15: Wisdom that is not from heaven—but is "earthly, unspiritual, demonic". This is the wisdom that we all naturally have—it's earthly.
2. Verse 17: "The wisdom that comes from heaven". This is true wisdom, which comes from outside this world, from God. It is something we have to ask for, and truly want to have as we ask for it (1 v 5-7).

• **What does each lead to?**
1. "Earthly wisdom" leads to envy and selfishness, and therefore to disorder and evil actions (v 14, 16). In other words, this wisdom is proud. It encourages us to promote ourselves and bring others down. And so living by this wisdom will of course lead to our words being negative, critical and destructive—whatever we would like to think.
2. "Heavenly wisdom" is seen not so much by our understanding and cleverness but by our deeds (v 13). Heavenly wisdom teaches us humility (because we know we don't have it naturally, and have had

to ask for it). And it leads (v 17) to purity, love of peace, being considerate and submissive and merciful, not being biased, and being sincere. Heavenly wisdom promotes selfless, relational peaceableness, which means that we "reap a harvest of righteousness" (v 17-18), both in our own lives as we live a life that pleases God; and in others as we promote and encourage them to be godly, or show them what the Christian life is like in an attractive way.

8. Why would verses 17-18 only be possible for someone who has a tight rein on their tongue? Promoting peace, being considerate, etc. will include how we use our tongues. Our actions will be undermined by our words if our words are still "on fire" from "hell" (v 6). So part of having true wisdom must include having a tight reign on our tongues, so that they speak increasingly only what is "wise".

9. Where was this fire from? From heaven—it is the Holy Spirit.

10. What is the connection between fire and speech (v 4, 11, see also v 14-22)? What did it prompt these Christians to do? Again, this fire leads to speech being produced; but here, it is speech that praises God and preaches Christ. The "spark" of the Spirit sets the tongue ablaze with praise for God and witness to his Son. In other words, this is heavenly wisdom in action.

11. APPLY: What is one mark of someone who is truly wise? That their tongues are full of praise for God and witness to Christ, and are not used to "curse" people made in God's image. Heavenly wisdom, given by the Father through the Spirit, will be seen in how someone talks.

12. APPLY: How can you encourage each other in how you use your tongues?
• **in what you do say.**
• **in what you don't say.**
There are no "wrong" answers here, but seek to be positive and practical. It could be as simple as asking each other whether we want to continue with a comment, or making space in your meetings to praise God and encourage one another, or praying for one another, for God to give heavenly wisdom. It may also include being accountable to someone else about our speech, i.e. inviting someone we trust to ask us each week whether and how we have spoken about God and about others.

5 James 4 v 1-12
HOW TO COME BACK TO GOD

THE BIG IDEA
Our conflicts and selfishness show that our hearts are spiritually adulterous towards God. Wonderfully, he extends grace to us if we are genuinely repentant.

SUMMARY
Conflict is part of everyday life, and comes in all sorts of contexts. And sadly, it does not cease at the door of the church. Our natural inclination, when we are caught up in conflict, is to blame others—but James locates the problem (or part of it) within us, not around us: quarrels "come from your desires that battle within you" (v 1). And conflicts show that we are not praying (v 2), but are self-reliant; or that we are praying but with wrong motives (v 3) because we are self-centred.

All this, James says, is a sign that his readers are "adulterous people" (v 4)—adulterous towards God because they are in love with the values of the world. James does not pull his punches: he defines sin (as much of the Old Testament does) as spiritual adultery towards the God who loves us and has rescued us.

This is why it is remarkable that God is still willing to love us and be in relationship with us—he calls us back and "gives us more grace" (v 6). He will show his "favour to the humble". In verses 7-9, James shows us what genuine repentance looks like— and much of the second half of this study considers what true repentance is, and encourages you to think about how much your own repentance looks like the genuine version that James lays out. Lastly, James shows us that Godward repentance will have

an impact on how we treat those around us—so in verse 11 he tells his "brothers and sisters" not to "slander one another". Genuine repentance for the (mis)use of tongues and our part in conflicts—and for the spiritual adultery that lies underneath those, and all sins—will mean a change of heart and of action.

So this is (again!) a very humbling study, showing us ourselves as we really are—but also one that gives us a greater appreciation of God's grace—that he goes on giving more forgiveness and kindness even to spiritual cheats such as us.

OPTIONAL EXTRA
Watch this modern-day dramatised presentation of the story of Hosea and Gomer (see Explore More). It is in six three-minute parts (if you are short of time, you could watch Parts 1, 3, 4 and 5). Type "Hosea Irving" into the search bar on youtube.

GUIDANCE FOR QUESTIONS
1. What, or who causes fights and quarrels:
• **in the workplace or the home?**
• **in church?**
It is possible the answers to both will be the same—because, as James will show us, what lies beneath conflicts is always the same— our selfish desires.

• **Think of a recent conflict you have been involved in, or witnessed. What happened? Why did it take place? Why did it continue?**

• **Why are churches so often undermined or split by conflicts, do you think?** Again, allow your group to come up with possibilities. Essentially, conflict does not stop at the door of the church because we tend as Christians not to be very different from those around us. Churches are groups of sinners, and we find it very easy to be directed by earthly "wisdom", which causes envy and division, rather than by heavenly wisdom, which leads to peace (remind your group of the previous study).

2. When we are involved in a quarrel, our instinct is to see the other person as the cause of the fight! But where does James locate the problem (v 1-2)? Conflicts "come from your desires that battle within you". The issue is not everybody else, but us. The problem is not out there; it is in here—in us. Conflict comes because our own selfish desires are not being met. James uses strong language; we might think he is being over the top—after all, we don't literally kill one another. But, as the Lord Jesus pointed out, we do not need to kill in order to commit a form of murder (Matthew 5 v 21-22).

☒

• **What kind of frustrated desires within us can cause, or continue, a conflict?** It might be the desire for status that leads us to vie for positions of influence and to envy others and do them down. It might be a desire to get even with someone who has hurt us, and so bitterness is nurtured over months and years. Or it could be the desire to protect ourselves from criticism that causes us to lash out at others pre-emptively.

3. When Christians act on their selfish desires, what are they forgetting (end v 2)? That God is generous (remember 1 v 5, 17-18), and that we are dependent on God. So "you do not have because you do not ask". When we are directed by our desires, we tend not to pray because we are wanting to run things our way, for our own sake. We decide what is good, and seek to gain it through our own efforts.

• **What else should Christians remember (v 3)?** That prayer is not a case of asking for something and God automatically granting the request. If we ask for something with "wrong motives"— here, to "spend what you get on your pleasures"—then we cannot expect God to give us what we ask for. For many of James' readers, prayer seems to have been a means of co-opting God into their plans; of using him to further their own purposes. When we allow the desires of our own hearts to grow unchecked, the result is a lack of answers to prayer—either because we become so engrossed in achieving our goals by our own means (and so do not come to God in prayer at all), or because we come to God treating him as the means to our own ends (and therefore praying with ungodly motives and intentions). If you don't see many answers to your prayers, maybe the problem is with your prayers!

4. How might praying, and praying according to God's priorities and not theirs, change the way James' first readers see their own desires, and their church conflicts? Because as we pray God-centred, God-honouring prayers, we become more aligned to his priorities, and less directed by our own desires. Part of the point of prayer is to remind ourselves of what God wants (think with your group about the Lord's Prayer—Luke 11 v 1-4—and the way it begins with God's concerns before moving onto ours). So James' readers, if they prayed with good motives, would begin to see their evil desires for what they were, and become less attached to and influenced by those desires. As they prayed for God's will to be done, rather than their own desires to be met, and as they prayed for wisdom (James 1 v 5, 3 v 17-18), they would seek peace, rather than conflict. James is telling them that the solution to conflicts is to pray, and pray in ways that please God.

5. What else does it show about us (v 4)?
That we have "adulterous" hearts. We are friends with the world (in other words, we desire to have what the world has, and live how the world lives); we are therefore enemies of God. **How do the words James chooses to use in verse 4 show us the seriousness of sin?** The imagery here is searing. We are to think of the horror of a husband or wife discovering their spouse in the midst of an affair. James says such horrendous behaviour aptly describes what Christians do when they turn their back on God and sin. This marital language is not original to James; the Old Testament commonly speaks of God coming to his people as a husband comes to his bride, and of his people responding in unfaithfulness to him (see Explore More). Christians two-time God when we adopt the values of the world. God takes it personally—just like a husband who finds his wife back in bed with the thug she was dating before he had come into her life and rescued her from that awful relationship. Such a husband would have every right to be angry. And James is very clear that being unfaithful to God provokes his enmity.

Note: James is not saying that being friends with people in the world is wrong; he is saying that friendship with the values of this world is wrong.

Note: Verse 5 is difficult to translate. It might be that by his Spirit God is jealous, or that he jealously longs for our spirit—our inner self—to be devoted. Either way, his concern and longing is that those who have wandered would return. The state of unfaithfulness that some of James' readers have got themselves into needs to end.

6. APPLY: In what ways are you (as a church and individually) most tempted to try to be friends with God and the world?
This is an opportunity for you to think about ways in which you as individuals and as a group of Christians are most likely to end up in friendship with the world. The ungodly values that you are most drawn to will depend on your surrounding culture—it could be materialism, or judgmentalism, or sexual immorality, or gluttony, or under/over respect for authority, or career-idolatry, or family-idolatry, and so on.

7. APPLY: How does thinking of sin as "spiritual adultery" change our view of:
• **ourselves?** We are not basically good, and we do not deserve to be God's people. Note that James is writing to Christians, and yet he calls them adulterous. We need to realise that our salvation rests on God's grace (v 6), and that we continue to be adulterous. This is very humbling.

• **our sins?** Sin is not a small thing. It is easy to excuse or belittle sin (or some sin, particularly the ones we commit); but every sin we commit is, spiritually, us being unfaithful to God. If we believed sin was spiritual adultery, we would be far keener to avoid it, and far more serious when we realise we have done it.

- **our temptations?** Temptations are invitations to cheat on God. They are the spiritual equivalent of a spouse considering whether to go to bed with someone they are not married to.

8. What truths about God does verse 6 contain?

1. "He gives us more grace." God wants his people back (v 5), and he will take his people back. He always stands ready to give us "grace", to love and forgive us.
2. He opposes the proud and favours the humble. Those who will not accept their need of him remain his enemies; those who accept and admit their sin, and its seriousness, are able to enjoy his favour.

Why is this amazing, considering the truth about us in verse 4? Because we are adulterers! God finds us in bed with the world, and yet he loves us enough to tell us to come back to him and to offer us forgiveness and restoration. And he goes on doing that! God does not give his grace to those who are "quite good"—he gives it to those who are, and continue to be, horrible.

EXPLORE MORE

Read Hosea 1 v 2-3; 3 v 1-6. Why is the prophet Hosea told to marry his wife, Gomer (1 v 2-3)? So that their marriage can be a human picture of the relationship between God and Israel, his people—he a loving husband; Israel is a cheating, unfaithful wife to him.

Why is Hosea told to restore his relationship with his wife (3 v 1)? Because that, too, will be a picture of God's treatment of his people. Hosea's wife is clearly now living with another man. But Hosea is to go and win her back and restore

their relationship, just as God will do for Israel despite their love for other gods.

What does it cost him (v 2)? Since Hosea is a picture of God, what are we meant to understand about his relationship with his people? Fifteen shekels of silver and about a homer and a lethek of barley. This was about a year's wages (CHECK)—a high price to pay. Again, we are pointed to God's treatment of his people—that his winning us back to be in relationship with him would come at a high price. It would cost his Son to free us from the consequences of our unfaithfulness so that we might live with him.

How is Hosea's marriage a powerful picture for us today about who we are and who God is? *Who we are:* as James has already told us, we are spiritual adulterers, loving other "gods" more than the God who made us and loves us.
Who God is: He is the One who has paid the ultimate price to buy us back, to free us to be his people again.

How does it move us to love God instead of the world? The world does not love us as God does and cannot fulfil us as he can. (Notice that the best Israel got from its other "gods" seems to have been "raisin cakes"!) But it is not the emptiness of the world that moves us to love God, but his love for us, seen most of all in the death of his Son in order to free us.

9. Trace out the stages of genuine repentance that James lays out (v 7-9).

- *Submit to God (v 7).* This means yielding to him, recognising his just and rightful rule over our lives. Submission is not an optional extra to the Christian life; it is part of what it means to relate to God rightly. And submitting means to submit our desires (v 1) to God—even asking him not to give us the things we deeply want when those things are deeply selfish.

- *Resist the devil (v 7)*. We acknowledge his influence, and determine not to be taken in by his lies. As we do this, James promises that "he will flee from you". We must not trivialise the power of Satan; but equally, we must not fear him. In a sense, it is as we submit to God that we resist the devil: they are two sides of the same thing.

- *Come near to God (v 8a)*. We admit how we have drifted, and we come back to loving and serving God. Again, James makes a promise: as we do this, "he will come near to you". God always stands ready to welcome us back.

- *Turn from sin (v 8b)*. We must change our behaviour and our thoughts ("hands … hearts", v 8b). Repentance involves a real change, a turn away from sin.

- *Feel the weight of our sin (v 9)*. Genuine repentance means that we grieve, even weep, about what we have done. James is not saying we can never be joyful (see 1 v 2). But there is a place for seriousness and grief about sin. If we are not more emotional about our sin (and salvation) than our sports team, or favourite film, or our children's ups and downs, there is something wrong.

- **How does the promise of verse 10 encourage us to genuinely repent?** Verses 6 and 10 both sum up the attitude of repentance mapped out in v 7-9 as being "humble". And as we show this, "he will lift you up". Gloom and grief are part of the genuine Christian response to sin, but they are not the totality of our Christian experience. God humbles us not to keep us down, but to lift us up. It is the contrite in heart that God esteems (Isaiah 66 v 2), and the poor in spirit who receive the kingdom of heaven (Matthew 5 v 3). Complacent laughter gives way to

mourning, and mourning now gives way to the joy of our salvation. There should be no people sadder, and yet happier, than Christians. The lower we are, the more lifted we are.

10. What does James say will be an outward sign that shows these Christians have really repented (v 11)? Not slandering one another. James is showing us that vertical repentance towards God has a horizontal dimension, too—it changes how we treat others. If James' readers repent of their destructive words (3 v 5-6) and of their destructive conflicts (4 v 1-3), caused by their desires and selfishness, then their behaviour will change.

11. APPLY: How similar, or different, is your usual view of repentance to James' explanation of real repentance here? Notice that repentance here is not simply saying "sorry", or feeling bad, or remembering we are forgiven, or being determined to do better, or saying a "catch-all" prayer in church once a week during the confession part of the service. **Which parts of genuine repentance do you find it easiest to forget or underplay, and why?** Go through your answers to Q9 and think about how each might look for the group.

12. APPLY: How will our Christian lives be damaged, possibly fatally, if we forget to live out any one of these verses?

- **v 4:** If we forget how horrendous sin is, we will not mind doing it; and we will be in danger of not truly repenting at all.

- **v 6:** If we forget how continual and amazing God's grace is, we will worry that he may stop loving us; we may even end up not asking him to forgive us because Satan convinces us that we have sinned one too many times for God to want us back.

- **v 7-9:** If we don't really believe the devil is active, or if we don't think we can resist him, then we will either give in to him without noticing, or live in fear of him. If we don't genuinely repent, we have not repented at all. It is only as we humble ourselves and weep over our sin that we can appreciate and sing about salvation.

- **How can you as a church help one another to believe and live by the truths and commands of these verses?** We should remember that sometimes we need to hear one of these truths more than another. But encourage your group not to belittle or explain away each other's sin, nor its seriousness; yet also to point each other to the ongoing grace that our Lord extends to us.

6 James 4 v 13 – 5 v 20
WISDOM IN PLANNING, PATIENCE IN SUFFERING

THE BIG IDEA
As we apply a gospel view of ourselves and the future to our planning and our sufferings, we'll be more humble and more patient. As Christians, it's our responsibility to call others back to living with genuine faith.

SUMMARY
In this final study, we see how to live lives of genuine faith in how we plan for the future, and when we suffer in the present.

Planning is unavoidable. But in 4 v 13-17, James shows us the danger of planning as though we were atheists. It is possible to plan with an ungodly, and in fact arrogant, attitude. So James reminds us (v 14-15) that we are not in control, and we are not the most significant person in the world. With this in mind, we will remember as we plan that "the Lord's will" (v 15) is what

matters—it must direct both how we plan (humbly) and what we plan (God's priorities must be our priorities).

In chapter 5, James turns to talk about how we respond to suffering, particularly when it is caused by someone else acting unjustly. First, he tells "you rich people" (most likely non-Christian rich people, see Q8)—who are pursuing wealth for its own sake, rather than using wealth for the sake of others, that "misery … is coming" (v 1). They have hoarded wealth, have used wealth to be extravagant, and have acted unjustly because of, and to increase, their wealth. It is not wealth that is the issue, but rather, what is done with it. James challenges us to check ourselves against his accusations.

But his main point comes in verses 7-12—"be patient" (v 7, 8). Because Jesus will return and bring justice, Christians who suffer injustice can wait patiently and faithfully. James points to the prophets as examples; they carried on their ministry faithfully while they were suffering (and were blessed, even though they were suffering). Then James points to Job, who was faithful in suffering and whom the Lord brought through that suffering.

Lastly, James returns to one of his favourite themes: prayer. He describes a range of circumstances a believer might face: "trouble … happy … ill" (v 13-14). In each case, the response is to pray. The details of v 14-16 are difficult, but the headline is simple: there is no situation in life where prayer to God is not relevant or right.

James finishes by commanding a "one another" ministry (v 19-20)—the ministry of seeking and calling Christians who are "wandering" from wholehearted faith to return. Our fellow Christians' wandering is not just their problem—it is our problem, too. Just as we seek to live lives shaped by genuine faith in Christ, so we are to encourage those who are struggling to continue in, or come back to, genuine faith, and live lives that reflect that faith.

Note: This study looks at a fairly long passage, and 5 v 13-18 is only covered in the Explore More section—so you could split the study into two at Q7 and take two sessions to cover the passage.

OPTIONAL EXTRA

Before the study, ask group members each to scribble down and bring with them what was on their home calendar or work schedule for the previous week, with names changed. To begin the session, read them out in turn, and ask group members to guess whose is whose. You could return to this after Q7 and encourage group members to think about what, if anything, would change on their calendars/schedules

if they remembered God's will in how they planned, and what they planned.

GUIDANCE FOR QUESTIONS

1. What does the way in which someone plans their schedule reveal about them spiritually, would you say?
• **What about the way in which someone responds to suffering?**
Allow the discussion to take its course in answer to these—you could return to the first part after Q5, and the second after Q10, to think about James' answers to these questions.

2. Who is James speaking to in these verses (v 13)? In the most specific sense, people who make plans regarding travelling and business. In James' day, merchants would have spent time in a new place, establishing contacts and trading before moving on somewhere else. But really, verse 13 is simply talking to people who make plans more generally—the details may differ, but plans like this are part and parcel of most of our lives. We all make plans, and think a year or so ahead. **What does their priority appear to be?** To "carry on business and make money". Profit is the motive for the planning. Again, this is not very different from many of our priorities today.

3. In verse 14, what does James want to remind the verse-13 people about:
• **the future?** They "do not even know what will happen tomorrow" (v 14a). None of us know what the immediate future holds. We are not in control of it, however much planning we do. We may put arrangements into the schedule as if they are a given (business trip, family holiday, seeing friends, starting a project), but James reminds us that we cannot

simply assume that once we've planned something, it will happen. We don't know the future.

- **themselves?** Each life, James says, is just "a mist that appears for a little while and then vanishes". We are not that important! We are around for a little while and then we vanish, just like the morning mist. James is reminding us that actually, in the grand scheme of things, we are not the centre of the universe, and we are not very significant.

4. What should they say instead? Verse 15: "If it is the Lord's will, we will live and do this or that". James is telling these people (and us) that there is nothing wrong with planning; but that we shouldn't plan in a way that forgets that God sovereignly overrules our lives. He is not telling us to add a mindless platitude to everything ("If it's God's will, then…") but to plan in a way that recognises and remembers that we are not in ultimate control, and that all our plans are subject to the will of God; and that we are not the centre of the universe or the most important person: God is.

5. How does verse 15 help us to see why verse 13 is, as James puts it, "arrogant", "boasting" and "evil" (v 16)? It is an arrogant view because it sees the future as under control, and the self as at the centre. It is "boasting" because it makes the person more important than they really are—and so it is "evil" because it forgets who God is. What seemed innocuous, sensible planning in verse 13 actually betrays an attitude that is vain, even "evil". This is very challenging to realise because often our planning is exactly like that of verse 13.

6. APPLY: Why is it good news that God is in charge of the future? Because, despite our planning and assumptions to the contrary, we are definitely not in charge (and we know this, deep down—it's why we don't trust weather forecasts!). One reason we struggle not to pretend we are in control is because deep down we then fear there would be no control. It is great news that there is someone in control, and that we know him to be both all-knowing and completely loving. And it is even greater news when we consider that God's purpose is to use our circumstances to make us more like Christ (1 v 3-5), and that he will definitely bring us through everything that lies in our future to bring us home to him (1 v 12; see Philippians 1 v 6). The purpose of this question is to help your group realise that God's control of our future is not oppressive, but liberating and encouraging.

7. APPLY: How should these verses affect both how we plan, and what we plan? *How we plan:* We will plan prayerfully and humbly, bearing in mind that God may direct our life differently, and asking him to help us to plan in a way that makes the wisest use of the time and opportunities he's given us.

What we plan: In the example of planning that James gives in verse 13, the planner's main aim is making money. Profit is the priority that drives the planning. It is not that making money is bad. It is what merchants do, after all. We would expect nothing different. But this is the point. If our planning is no different from that of the world around us, what does that say about our faith in Christ? It is not wrong for making some money to be a goal in life— we are to support ourselves and help others. But it is wrong for it to be our main goal in life. Our plans need to reflect not only the existence of God's will, but its content too.

We need to make plans that enable us to do the "good" we're called to do (v 17). So if our plans mean that we are irregular in church attendance, or have no time to care for the vulnerable, or rarely listen to God in his word, then there must be some sin in our planning.

8. Who is James speaking to in verses 1-6? The simple answer is "you rich people" (v 1). But there is good reason for thinking James is addressing non-Christian rich people. Notice that in these verses James does not address those he's speaking to as "brothers and sisters" or "fellow believers", which he does liberally through the rest of the letter (e.g. 1 v 16; 2 v 1, 14; 3 v 1; 4 v 11). And there is no call to repent and return to the Lord, but only a promise of judgment.

Why would James address the unbelieving rich, since they won't be in a church to hear his words?! Because (like the prophets often did) James is not wanting to teach those he is addressing, but to show his Christian hearers what God thinks of those he is addressing. In other words, James wants Christians to know how to think of the rich people around them in a godly way.

- **And what does he warn them about?**
  - v 2-3: They have amassed and hoarded wealth for its own sake, rather than using their wealth for good. But it has not done them any good, and it "testifies against" them—it exposes the sinfulness of hearts that aimed simply to have wealth, rather than to use wealth.
  - v 4: They have used their wealth to take advantage of and exploit others, and God sees and cares about that (see also v 6).
  - v 3b, 5: They have done all this "in the last days". In other words, the day of God's judgment is coming and is not far off, and yet they have lived for possessions in the here and now. Like turkeys eating well in October, but heading all the while for Christmas, so living for wealth now and treading on others to get more of it simply means people have "fattened [themselves] in the day of slaughter" (v 5).

In summary, God warns that the hoarding, the injustice and the extravagance by which these people have lived all expose a heart that is sinful and will bring God's judgment.

⊗

- **How might we end up living like the people James takes aim at here?** As we've seen, James is speaking to non-Christian wealthy people—but it is very easy for us to treat wealth in a non-Christian way, rather than ensuring that our faith impacts our deeds in this area. *Hoarding:* In the West, we live in a society where accumulation is seen as good in its own right. Amassing money and possessions is commended. It is one of the ways that we as a culture measure someone's success in life. The more you have, the better you've done. The things we have are a matter of pride to many of us, rather than seen as something that we are to use to bless others. *Injustice:* We may not be negligent landowners, as these people evidently were, but this still hits home. It is all too easy for the wealthy to overlook the needs of others and their responsibility to them. Affluence can lead to carelessness and insensitivity. Moreover, those of us in the comparative wealth of the West need to reflect on our responsibility as consumers—to think about the kinds of companies we're supporting and how they treat their workers in far-flung and impoverished places. Wilful ignorance really is no defence. Our purchasing habits might well be furthering forms of injustice, and we have an opportunity to make a difference through the choices that we make. It is incumbent on us to care about such things and to do all we can to support upright companies and avoid those that deliberately hurt and exploit the economically vulnerable.

Extravagance: The Bible does not say we cannot enjoy good things (1 Timothy 4 v 1-5). But we are not to aim for the most comfortable, pampered life possible; nor should we live envying the rich for their extravagance.

9. Why should Christians be "patient and stand firm" when they suffer or are exploited (v 7-9)? In answering this, direct your group first to the verses just looked at. Cries of injustice do reach God's ears (v 4), and there will be judgment of those who have used their power to exploit others (v 5). The unjust will not get away with it.

Then look at verses 7-9. James reinforces this point: "Be patient ... until the Lord's coming" which "is near" (v 7, 8). Then he repeats the point: "The Judge is standing at the door!" (v 9)—the Lord Jesus is within earshot, and could "come in" at any moment. And his coming will herald the judgment of all sin and the righting of all wrongs. Christians are not called to endless patience, but patience with hope, with an end in sight. We are to wait patiently and faithfully until the day we know is coming, and the day we know could be today.

10. What examples does James point us to, and what point is he making with each?

- **v 7:** A farmer. In Israel, rain came twice a year (Oct/Nov and March/April). Between these times, the farmer might need regularly to tend the ground and keep the weeds at bay, but he could do nothing at all to accelerate the process of bringing the crops to harvest. He had to wait. He knew the rain would come, and with it the harvest. It would happen, but it had not yet happened. He just needed to exercise patience—to wait with confidence. (If you have time, read Deuteronomy 11 v 13-14.) James is making a theological point—the farmer has to wait for the rain that is provided by God at just the right time; we are to wait for the justice that is provided by God at just the right time.

- **v 10-11a:** The prophets. First, they show us that suffering is not novel; it has been the lot of God's people throughout the generations. Second, they show that it is possible to serve God (in their case they "spoke in the name of the Lord") even while suffering—we're not to think we can't serve God until things get easier. Third, suffering does not mean we are not blessed—after all, "we count as blessed those who have persevered" (v 11) despite great suffering.

- **v 11b:** Job. (If your group don't know the story well, explain that Job lost everything—his possessions, family and health—yet remained faithful, and in the end God restored everything and more to him.) Job shows us that it is worth patiently persevering. One day, God will give us even more than he gave Job: the "crown of life" (1 v 12).

EXPLORE MORE
How should Christians respond to:
- **trouble?** Pray.
- **happiness?** Pray.

• **sickness?** Pray.

Note: Verses 14-16 are very hard to understand. My reading of them is that James is talking about situations where sickness may be part of God's discipline on someone who is sinning unrepentantly—so they require prayer to "make [them] well" (v 15), and therefore James encourages Christians to confess their sins to each other (v 16).

So these verses are *not* teaching:

• the Roman Catholic practice of last rites—in James 5, the sick individual recovers, rather than dies.

• that we should hold healing rallies—James talks about ministry happening in a home, and those praying are normal elders, not special "healers".

• that prayer will *always* lead to healing—in the Bible, godly people are sometimes not healed (eg: 1 Timothy 5 v 23).

• that this is only about spiritual sickness (ie: weak faith), not physical sickness—if James had meant weak faith, he would have surely said so!

Do allow your group to spend time discussing these verses, but don't allow it to dominate your time together, or the applications for your group. For more detail on this, see *James For You*, pages 149-155.

How does Elijah's example encourage us to do this (v 16b-18)? Eljiah was a human being, just like us. Yet he was a "righteous person" (see v 16)—so he prayed for God to judge sinfulness (that it would not rain, and it did not—see 1 Kings 17 v 1, 7); and he prayed for God to bless his repentant people (to send rain, and God did—see 1 Kings 18 v 16-46). So Elijah is an example of a man who prayed godly prayers, and those prayers changed things. As we pray in line with God's priorities, we can know that our prayers truly are "powerful and effective" (James 5 v 16), just as his were.

11. APPLY: How might you spot "wandering" when it comes to scheduling and suffering? Share suggestions, but how people spend their time and what people say about their lives are two great indicators of wandering, e.g. if someone is rarely in church, then their scheduling suggests a wandering heart; if someone speaks bitterly or only ever joylessly about a trial they are facing, and never mentions the Lord as they speak about it, that may well be a sign of a wandering heart.

• **How committed are you to bringing people back?** Trying to call a wanderer back to genuine faith is not easy; it can feel incredibly awkward, and it can be unpopular both with that person and with other members of our church. So we do need consciously to commit to noticing and lovingly challenging those who are wandering. **What would that look like?** This will depend on the characters of those involved, and the way in which they are wandering, but at the least it must mean speaking—humbly, lovingly and gently, but also clearly and firmly—and praying. The purpose of this part of the question is for your group to talk in practical ways, rather than remaining at the level of "good intentions" that never turn into real action.

12. APPLY: Think back through the whole of the letter of James. What has he shown you a life of genuine faith looks like? What have you, as a group, found most challenging? Encourage your group to spend some time quietly thinking this through on their own, before you share answers.

Good Book Guides
The full range

OLD TESTAMENT

Exodus: 8 Studies
Tim Chester
ISBN: 9781784980269

Judges: 6 Studies
Timothy Keller
ISBN: 9781908762887

Ruth: 4 Studies
Tim Chester
ISBN: 9781905564910

David: 6 Studies
Nathan Buttery
ISBN: 9781904889984

1 Samuel: 6 Studies
Tim Chester
ISBN: 9781909919594

2 Samuel: 6 Studies
Tim Chester
ISBN: 9781784982195

1 Kings 1–11: 8 Studies
James Hughes
ISBN: 9781907377976

Elijah: 5 Studies
Liam Goligher
ISBN: 9781909559240

Esther: 7 Studies
Jane McNabb
ISBN: 9781908317926

Psalms: 6 Studies
Tim Chester
ISBN: 9781904889960

Psalms: 7 Studies
Christopher Ash & Alison Mitchell
ISBN: 9781784984182

Proverbs: 8 Studies
Kathleen Nielson & Rachel Jones
ISBN: 9781784984304

Ezekiel: 6 Studies
Tim Chester
ISBN: 9781904889274

Daniel: 7 Studies
David Helm
ISBN: 9781910307328

Hosea: 8 Studies
Dan Wells
ISBN: 9781905564255

Jonah: 6 Studies
Stephen Witmer
ISBN: 9781907377433

Micah: 6 Studies
Stephen Um
ISBN: 9781909559738

Zechariah: 6 Studies
Tim Chester
ISBN: 9781904889267

NEW TESTAMENT

Mark 1–8: 10 Studies
Tim Chester
ISBN: 9781904889281

Mark 9–16: 7 Studies
Tim Chester
ISBN: 9781904889519

Luke 1–12: 8 Studies
Mike McKinley
ISBN: 9781784980160

Luke 12–24: 8 Studies
Mike McKinley
ISBN: 9781784981174

Luke 22–24: 6 Studies
Mike McKinley
ISBN: 9781909559165

John: 7 Studies
Tim Chester
ISBN: 9781907377129

John 1-12: 8 Studies
Josh Moody
ISBN: 9781784982188

John 13-21: 8 Studies
Josh Moody
ISBN: 9781784983611

Acts 1-12: 8 Studies
R. Albert Mohler
ISBN: 9781910307007

Acts 13-28: 8 Studies
R. Albert Mohler
ISBN: 9781910307014

Romans 1–7: 7 Studies
Timothy Keller
ISBN: 9781908762924

Romans 8–16: 7 Studies
Timothy Keller
ISBN: 9781910307311

1 Corinthians 1–9:
7 Studies
Mark Dever
ISBN: 9781908317681

1 Corinthians 10–16:
8 Studies
Mark Dever & Carl Laferton
ISBN: 9781908317964

1 Corinthians:
8 Studies
Andrew Wilson
ISBN: 9781784986254

2 Corinthians:
7 Studies
Gary Millar
ISBN: 9781784983895

Galatians: 7 Studies
Timothy Keller
ISBN: 9781908762566

Ephesians: 10 Studies
Thabiti Anyabwile
ISBN: 9781907377099

Ephesians: 8 Studies
Richard Coekin
ISBN: 9781910307694

Philippians: 7 Studies
Steven J. Lawson
ISBN: 9781784981181

Colossians: 6 Studies
Mark Meynell
ISBN: 9781906334246

1 Thessalonians:
7 Studies
Mark Wallace
ISBN: 9781904889533

1&2 Timothy: 7 Studies
Phillip Jensen
ISBN: 9781784980191

Titus: 5 Studies
Tim Chester
ISBN: 9781909919631

Hebrews: 8 Studies
Justin Buzzard
ISBN: 9781906334420

Hebrews: 8 Studies
Michael J. Kruger
ISBN: 9781784986049

James: 6 Studies
Sam Allberry
ISBN: 9781910307816

1 Peter: 6 Studies
Juan R. Sanchez
ISBN: 9781784980177

1 John: 7 Studies
Nathan Buttery
ISBN: 9781904889953

Revelation: 7 Studies
Tim Chester
ISBN: 9781910307021

TOPICAL

Man of God: 10 Studies
Anthony Bewes & Sam
Allberry
ISBN: 9781904889977

Biblical Womanhood:
10 Studies
Sarah Collins
ISBN: 9781907377532

The Apostles' Creed:
10 Studies
Tim Chester
ISBN: 9781905564415

**Promises Kept: Bible
Overview:** 9 Studies
Carl Laferton
ISBN: 9781908317933

The Reformation Solas
6 Studies
Jason Helopoulos
ISBN: 9781784981501

Contentment: 6 Studies
Anne Woodcock
ISBN: 9781905564668

Women of Faith:
8 Studies
Mary Davis
ISBN: 9781904889526

Meeting Jesus: 8 Studies
Jenna Kavonic
ISBN: 9781905564460

Heaven: 6 Studies
Andy Telfer
ISBN: 9781909919457

Making Work Work:
8 Studies
Marcus Nodder
ISBN: 9781908762894

The Holy Spirit: 8 Studies
Pete & Anne Woodcock
ISBN: 9781905564217

Experiencing God:
6 Studies
Tim Chester
ISBN: 9781906334437

Real Prayer: 7 Studies
Anne Woodcock
ISBN: 9781910307595

Mission: 7 Studies
Alan Purser
ISBN: 9781784983628

thegoodbook

COMPANY

BIBLICAL | RELEVANT | ACCESSIBLE

At The Good Book Company, we are dedicated to helping Christians and local churches grow. We believe that God's growth process always starts with hearing clearly what he has said to us through his timeless word—the Bible.

Ever since we opened our doors in 1991, we have been striving to produce Bible-based resources that bring glory to God. We have grown to become an international provider of user-friendly resources to the Christian community, with believers of all backgrounds and denominations using our books, Bible studies, devotionals, evangelistic resources, and DVD-based courses.

We want to equip ordinary Christians to live for Christ day by day, and churches to grow in their knowledge of God, their love for one another, and the effectiveness of their outreach.

Call us for a discussion of your needs or visit one of our local websites for more information on the resources and services we provide.

Your friends at The Good Book Company

thegoodbook.com | thegoodbook.co.uk
thegoodbook.com.au | thegoodbook.co.nz
thegoodbook.co.in